Dimes From Heaven

Dimes From Heaven

How Coins and Coincidences Helped Me Discover My Life as an Empath

Monica L. Morrissey

Lindsey Menard

Monica L. Morrissey LLC

Dedication

To My Husband, Brian, our two sons, Shamus and Patrick, our two Grandsons, Lincoln and Jackson and any other future Grandchildren I may have some day. Thank you for always loving me just as I am. May you always believe in the things that you do not see.

I have tried to recreate events, locales and conversations from my memories of them. These memories are from my perspective only. Others may or may not remember them as I do.

"Yet winks from God are not communication to those who die; they are messages to the living, providing reassurance that the person who died has a role to play in the infinite plan and that those of us who are left have a continued role here on earth."~ SQuire Rushnell ~ When God Winks

Acknowledgements

I want to thank my husband first. If he hadn't planted the seed about this story becoming a book, I might never have followed through with it. He always knew how sensitive I was but I never wanted to admit it. Thank you for loving me and understanding that I had to follow my dreams.

A big thank you to both of my children, Shamus and Patrick, for being who they are and helping me become a better person. I feel blessed to be your Mom. Thank you to the two women who love my boys, Emily and Heather. You both chose to love my kids and for that I am so grateful to have you as part of our family.

Thank you to my older sister, Debbie. You are always there for me no matter what. I know Mom and Dad are always with you too.

Thank you to Victoria Hill, who gave me permission to tell my story. You listened to my first draft (which sucked by the way!) and gave me the courage to face my fears. You took time out of your busy life to sit on my front porch, take a hike up Barr Hill and listen to my story. You weren't afraid to tell me the truth that I needed to hear. You gave me the confidence to continue writing, even when it was difficult.

Thank you to Tracy and Chelsea Collier. Tracy helped me to "show don't tell" in my writing; which is something I used to teach to my students. Chelsea- I loved how you turned into my teacher and I was the student. You both gave me great advice, especially when I was stuck. I feel honored to call you my friends, my soulmates.

Thank you to my dear friend, Tanya Barber, who helped me enjoy life everyday. Thank you for being there when my anxiety was at its most extreme. I had no idea how difficult writing was going to be. You were there to lend an ear and some advice. I am forever grateful for our friendship and our memorable trips to Wal-mart and Olive Garden with our husbands!

Thank you to Kim Knudson who helped me with editing. You were my editor in chief just like when our students wrote the Greensboro History books. You questioned me and made me explain things so that it would be easier to understand. I enjoyed talking with you during our many meetings!

Thank you to Wendy for reading my manuscript and giving me tips on how to organize my sentences. I appreciate your friendship and you support!

Thank you to all of the healers who have helped me work through so many different emotions and physical issues. Thank you to Betty who helped me work through my present life through past life regression work and EFT. My acupuncturist, Sarah, and my massage therapist, Liv, who both listened to me when I lost both of my parents. Along with helping my body heal from the stress, you helped me emotionally and I can never thank you enough. Thank you to Michelle, who helped me with my digestion when the medical doctors couldn't. You helped me find my "qi"(pronounced chee) when I didn't know it was gone. Thank you to Sierra who helped me find the pieces of my soul that I had lost throughout my life. I will never forget you saying, "Welcome back Monica." I felt it inside my entire body. Thank you to Grace, who first helped me heal after my back surgery. You gave me my life back. I am honored to now have you all as friends. Without you, this book never would have been possible.

Thank you to my new "parents" who make me feel loved everyday. I feel blessed to be a part of my Uncle David and Aunt Jean's life. You both helped me and Dad when Mom passed away. I know that my Mom and Dad are thankful for your continued support after they left us. Thank you to Eldon, who always reminds me how important God is in our lives and how God heals us. I am blessed to have you in my life. Thank you to Merrilee for caring for my father and adopting me after both of my parents transitioned to Spirit. When I receive love from the four of you, I imagine that you are also giving me love from my parents. You are my angels and I am blessed to have you all in my life.

Thank you to all of our friends who feel like family. As I danced with my son on his wedding day this year, I felt the love from all of you to my entire family. The Morrisseys feel blessed to have you in our lives.

Thank you to our Dimick Road family. Brian and I had no idea how special it would be to raise our family surrounded by all of you. I am so thankful that we moved to Dimick Road and our kids had such good people around them while they were growing up. You all are a part of our hearts forever and always.

Thank you to all of my students. Whenever I talk about "my kids", I would have to distinguish between my own children and my students. All of my students will always be "my kids" because I got to be a part of your lives for a time period. I loved teaching and our time together will always be a part of me. I love connecting with each and every one of you on Facebook or in person. I hope that some of you may write a book someday!

Thank you to Terhas, who said to me one time, "I love how your heart is so open." It's open with you Terhas, because I know that I can trust you and you won't hurt me. I'm not like that with everyone. Both of my parents loved you too. I look forward to reading your memoir someday.

Thank you to all of my colleagues, especially the ones who helped me during the time I lost both of my parents and the ones who encouraged me to write my dime story. I feel honored to work with you and know that you all are making a difference in the lives of many children. Thank you for choosing to be an educator. It can be one of the most challenging but also the most rewarding job you will ever have. To Sylvia, who, when I told her I was going to write a book, was just as excited as I was! You are a beautiful soul.

I know so many people who have been affected by the death of a loved one. I hope that my dime story will help all of us understand and know that our loved ones are near us every single day. I know it isn't the same living life without them, but I hope we all feel love in our hearts from Heaven.

Thank you especially to my Mom and Dad. I know you were with me every step of the way. It wasn't "goodbye" when you left me, it was "See you later."

There are so many people in my life that I am thankful for. This book was one of the most difficult things I have ever done in my life. It is most definitely my Baby and I hope you enjoy it as much as I have enjoyed sharing my story with you.

Note from the author

I always knew that I had a deeper connection to something. I wasn't sure how to explain it and I didn't always know how to access it. Looking back now, I realize that I wasn't raised to explore or understand this connection and it went against everything that I felt inside. This story is my journey about discovering the world beyond the human experience and learning to accept my gifts and challenges as an empath. I didn't set out to write a memoir. I only wanted to write about the dimes. I didn't know that through the process of writing, I would heal from the inside out. Before I did that though, I had to understand my life from a different perspective. I had to step out of my anger and into my body. That's when I found the answers. This book shares the intimate details of how being an empath affected every part of my life, including food, relationships, and my internal messages to myself. The Liberty Head dimes helped me have "Freedom of Thought", which is the meaning of that particular dime. May you have Freedom of Thought as you read.

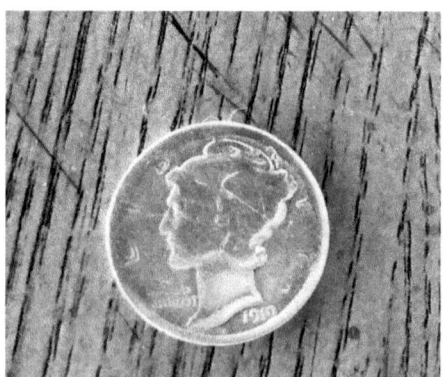

"A memoirists work is not just to transcribe his life, but to uncover meaning behind those life experiences for himself, and for his readers." ~ Joni B. Cole

Connect with me!
Facebook @monicalmorrissey and Dimes from Heaven group
Website: www.monicalmorrissey@gmail.com

Foreword

I have been privileged to be a part of Monica Morrissey's healing journey for over a decade, ever since she sought me out for a past life regression some time ago. Years might go by between our times of connecting, but at crucial moments Monica would always show up to face herself honestly, dig deeply, and heal what needed healing so that she could claim more and more of her authentic self.

It is a joy to hold this book in my hands. How beautiful to see Monica not only claim the truth of who she is as an empath, but also share her story with the world. It is one thing to work deeply on one's own healing and become more whole, and I have such respect for anyone who takes this journey. It is quite another to have the courage to share this intimate journey through writing. We are so fortunate that Monica has felt this calling to share her experiences.

When Monica first told me the stories of the dimes, I thought, "These stories must be shared!" They are remarkable evidence that the love and connection do not end with physical death. As Brian Weiss says, only love is real. These experiences are a testimony to that truth. Inspiring, reassuring, tangible proof – I love these stories from Monica's direct experience.

While the "dimes from heaven" are the core of the book, the reader will find much more in these pages. Monica lets us into her life as she describes the challenge it has been to grow up as an empath in a family and culture where feelings were not affirmed or encouraged; where her gift of sensitivity was ignored and thus hidden for so long; where, at ag 50, "coming out" as her true self still feels perilous. How many readers will relate to this? Many, I believe. In my practice, I work with so many highly sensitive people whose lives have been marked by the fear of begin who they really are. This speaks to me personally as well.

And so this book is a gift to us all. The many authors who have helped Monica find her way are quoted throughout the book. Monica Morrissey is, after all, a professional educator and part of her mission is to share information and resources. Readers will benefit from the extensive bibliography at the end and will find much valuable and inspirational information.

We often hear that the two primary emotions which underlie all others are Love and Fear. Indeed, we can often feel how we vacillate between the two, longing to open our hearts but fearful of being hurt or unsafe. It is author Gary Zukav who added a nuance that I have appreciated: we either choose Love or Trust, or we let Fear and Doubt prevail.

I have been so moved by Monica Morrissey's honesty and vulnerability as, over and over, she faces her own fears and doubts and shares this part of the journey as well. It is deeply human and remarkably open-hearted. And then, despite the struggle, she finds ways to cultivate more love and trust and keep affirming what she believes and knows. Her process, described in detail in the book, is a real inspiration.

The world feels like a dangerous place for empaths and highly sensitive people. And yet the world so needs their gifts of sensitivity and spiritual connection. It is an act of great courage to bring a book like this into being. Thank you, Monica, for trusting us with your story and yourself. We are the richer for it.

Betty Moore-Hafter
Certified Hypnotherapist and EFT Master Trainer
Certified in Past Life Regression by Dr. Brian Weiss
https:/creativeeft.com
Author of *Freedom at Your Fingertips,* along with nineteen other World Class EFT experts

"I believe in Healing. I believe deeply that the key to healing our lives and achieving our goals is inside each of us. We can rediscover our "blueprint" for wholeness and well-being within the deep inner self. I think of myself as a companion on the journey, a partner in healing, and I approach that role with compassion and non-judgment. I bring to you my

deepest listening and presence, and I trust your own healing process that is unfolding. This is a privilege for which I am very grateful.

__Are You a Seeker Too?__ In some ways, we are all seekers, aren't we? Seeking happiness, seeking relief from pain, seeking fulfilling relationships, seeking a satisfying life. I wanted to understand what blocks our wholeness and how we can heal and be more in alignment with our best selves, even when the going is rough and challenges and adversity come our way."

Betty Moore-Hafter

__I am forever thankful that I was able to work with Betty. May the readers of this book seek to find the answers within you. ~Monica__

Preface

"The essential lesson I've learned in life is to just be yourself. Treasure the magnificent being that you are and recognize first and foremost you're not here as a human being only. You're a spiritual being having a human experience." ~Wayne Dyer

Over the past ten years or so, I noticed more and more people talking about signs from people who have transitioned to spirit. I wanted with all of my heart to believe in such a thing. A voice inside me questioned and doubted everything that I couldn't prove. *How could this be true? I wondered.* Ever since I was a little girl I wanted to believe that there was only good in the world and God would help those who were hurt. During some of the chaotic moments and events in my life, I lost pieces of myself. I was trying now, as I was about to turn **50**, to discover where my soul's journey was going to take me next. My body was sending me messages to change and grow, but I struggled accepting myself. Through writing, I was able to dig deep, get clear, and heal in a very different way than I ever imagined. Through writing, I discovered I was an empath, something I knew very little about. It was my life lesson to learn to be me, exactly the way God made me. To do that though, I had to question the foundation of my childhood.

"Then I realized, what do they really know? This is MY idea, I thought. No one knows it like I do. And it's ok if it is different, and weird, and maybe a little crazy. I decided to protect it, to care for it. I fed it good food, I worked with it. I played with it. But, most of all, I gave it my attention." ~Kobi Yamada from What Do You Do with an Idea?

Here is **my** story; the first "phone call" and the many dimes my father sent from Heaven.

Table of Contents:

1 |

Chapter 1 My Young Life

More Than a Dime

"I learned from my journey that a true seeker must go deep into his or her own consciousness to come closer to realizing the truth of our existence." ~Eben Alexander M.D.

Chapter 1 My Young Life

"More learning can occur when there are many obstacles than when there are few or none. A life with difficult relationships, filled with obstacles and losses, presents the most opportunity for the

soul's growth. You may have chosen the more difficult life so that you could accelerate your physical progress." ~Brian Weiss

Monica L. Morrissey

My first memory of talking to angels was when I was maybe 10 or 11. I can remember being so un-happy in my family that I started to "talk" to the lights floating outside my bedroom window. *Does everyone have a voice inside their head that speaks to them? Where does it come from? Does it only come from my brain? Does it come from someplace else? Do other people think about things as much as I do? I won-der as I speak to the floating lights outside my window. I'm on the top bunk, mostly because I am the "big" sister. If I didn't have to sleep on the top bunk, I never would have seen the lights. It's almost like they are talking to me, supporting me when I feel alone. Who are they I wonder? I feel like they like me.* During those years on the top bunk, I stared at the floating balls of light in the corner of the house every night. They were like bubbles that never popped. *Why would I think that I could talk to them?* Because of the dimes, I would begin to understand the **things we cannot see and my own connection to spirits.**

Some of my childhood memories are blank; blocked out. There were times in my life that were great and others that were more difficult. During the difficult times, I would put on a mask and pretend I was ok. I didn't have the strength to live like others. I was sensitive and didn't know how to express any of my feelings. For me, when my mother spoke to me about something I had done wrong, I didn't know how to recover from it. I would feel so bad. It was like the words got stuck in-side my body and then I didn't feel good. I thought that because of the way she had spoken to me, she might not love me anymore. *My family didn't understand me, either. Most of the time I didn't know what to do. I wanted to talk about feelings and it seemed my parents wanted me to 'get over it'.* Because of this, I learned how to hide all of my feelings, stuffing them all inside my body and eventually this made me sick.

My cousin's husband says he thinks I was a UPS kid- dropped off in a family where I didn't belong. I laughed but knew how true this felt. *Anita Moorjani describes this feeling perfectly in her book, Dying to Be Me, "Why am I always different, wherever I go? Where do I belong? Why don't I feel like I belong anywhere?"* Although for different reasons, I think she understands how I felt. I believe she was confused because she didn't agree with all of the organized religious beliefs of her family and culture. This feeling seemed to create a war within her. *Does everyone feel this way? Does everyone want to belong somewhere? Why are there so many rules about believing in God? Can't we all believe in the same thing? Was my family the reason I needed to talk to the lights? Is this why I needed to know that someone else was out there, ready to love me for who I am?*

Growing up, I spent a lot of time outdoors. I loved to swim in the lake all summer and play outdoors in the woods. At my family's camp on the lake, I would catch frogs, fish, water ski and play out on the raft with my friends. The lake I swam in was filled with mud and seaweed, but I didn't

care. Some girls I know wouldn't even go near a lake like that. I was a tomboy at heart and I

remember wanting to live in the woods. For me, these times outside seemed magical. Growing up in the 70's, we would play outside until it was dark. We were up and down the street at different houses until the day was done. I loved to be outside.

Our family camp on Lake Elmore was a magical place for everyone. I learned to water ski when I was five years old. I still have the red, white and blue striped skis that I got for Christmas one year. I would go out in the row boat and fish with my Grandmother. At night, we played kick the can. My cousins had a camp three down from our camp so we would all get together to play when it got dark. The boundaries were the road, the lake and in between about five camps. I was one of the younger kids and I'm sure I was outsmarted most of time.

As an adult, I enjoy spending time outside- hiking, camping, or swimming. I once had a friend who I met in my late thirties, say to me, "With you, I have done the most things outside, without make-up, that I have ever done in my entire life!" Yup, that is me- an outside, no make-up kinda gal! Hiking and being in nature gives me time to think. I can start a hike ruminating on something going on in my life and by the end of the hike, I have worked through it. It's almost like when I work out and sweat on the hike it clears out the negative thinking. If only I could hike everyday. Of course, my favorite hike is Elmore Mountain, directly across from the family camp on the lake. When I hike that mountain, I feel like I am home. *I feel connected.*

For people who know me professionally, they might wonder about the person I described. "What? Monica always shows up to school with her nails done, wears dresses and always looks great. She can't be a tomboy or a nature freak!" Truth be told, if I had a choice, I would be in yoga pants and a t-shirt every single day living out in the woods. For my profession though, I have to be able to get up and go to work every day. I believe that as an educator, I have to show up to work looking professional. Except for make-up- I still do not wear make-up. People will see my real face every day.

We had an electric player piano and a pool table in the basement at our house. All the kids would head downstairs to play. We would sit on the bench at the piano and sing along to songs like Mickey Mouse March, John Denver's Country Roads, Take me Home or If I Were a Rich man from the play Fiddler on the Roof. If we weren't singing songs we were playing pool, hide and seek or a variety of board games. Whenever I had sleepovers, we always slept in the basement. We always had to be super quiet. I was always embarrassed when my mom would holler down the stairs. When she flicked the lights, it either meant quiet down or dinner was ready. I was never sure which one she was going to say.

We had a sugar house out back and it was up to the kids to help gather the sap. We would ride all over to different sugarwoods in the back of a pick up truck. We had to carry five gallon buckets to gather the sap. There was one family in particular who always helped our family with making syrup. Having them there made it so much more fun. When it would get late in the spring, the sap would be yellow and sometimes we would find mice in the buckets. Although that part wasn't always fun, the best part was when the Mom of the family who helped us would bake maple biscuits. The yummy taste of maple syrup would make all the hard work worth it.

These recollections could go on and on. This is long before electronics took over our world. Of course, these are all great memories for me, but I felt lost in the crowd. I didn't feel like I fit in. I was too sensitive and had difficulty "being tough". These memories most likely create such a happy feeling for everyone who was there. When I think of the time spent with all the different families we were friends with, it was most definitely the best part of my childhood.

From the outside looking in, my young life most likely looked fine to most people. I was a pretty girl (at least that is what people told me- of course, I didn't feel 'pretty'), our family had lots of friends and relatives around, I got good grades, and had plenty of friends at school. Many people will reminisce about the fun times they had at our house and our family camp on Lake Elmore. To them, our family probably looked a lot like Leave it to Beaver. Everything was good on the outside and inside. To me, I knew that something wasn't right. I could feel it inside me. *Was it me or was it the family I was born into? How would I ever have the courage to look inside myself to find who I truly am? Sometimes I feel like I am fighting voices in my head, wondering if I am enough. How can I feel like I am enough?*

I spoke to lights. *Crazy, right?* At a very young age, my mother didn't understand who I was. Growing up, I always felt it was important to keep up appearances. It seemed important to my Mom to make sure people thought our family was perfect, a fact that would make me struggle to share any of my feelings with anyone. As an adult in my 20's, 30's and most of my 40's, this is how I would also live my life- thinking and worrying about what other people thought about me and my family. I knew I needed to learn that there was a different way to live.

I would never have dared to share this information with anyone- *and now I am putting all of this on paper! Somebody might read it, my truth would be revealed...my mother's voice worries me as I write. I am putting myself in a very vulnerable position, one which I had tried my whole life to cover up. I needed to learn how to live differently. Making mistakes was ok. Being imperfect was ok.*

"Owning our story and loving ourselves through that process is the bravest thing that we will ever do." ~Brene Brown.

Brene Brown, through all of her books, created such a different role model for me to learn to live differently. She talked and shared all of her feelings. This was something new for me. I thought I had to stuff all of my feelings to look tough. I thought I had to be different on the outside and couldn't share what I was feeling on the inside.

Growing up, we attended church, but I never felt God in our house. In fact, it was the opposite. For our house, I felt church wasn't about living with God's message; it was about putting on an air that we were a strong family. I felt that church made us look good. I remember the minister visiting my father, soon after my mother's passing. She tried to explain to me that she didn't really understand my Mom and that they "had an understanding". I got it. I knew exactly what she was saying. I had an understanding with my Mom also, and that was to not explore what made me who I am or to talk about any other "nonsense". Emotions, God and talking about our problems would all be off limits. *'Just suck it up and deal with it,' I would think to myself. I guess having four children to deal with, there wasn't much time to help me deal with my insecurities, or other such silly things, like not making the softball team.*

Why did I struggle every time my parents spoke to me about a mistake I had made? Why did I worry so much? As a child and a teenager, there were many things that happened to me that I never dared to talk to anyone about. I was always worried what other people would think. I did turn to God though. I thought He would always listen to me and love me. At least, that is what I believed.

People have a lot of different words for God, Spirit, Jesus, etc. For me, God is a Spirit with an all encompassing positive energy field around everything in the entire universe. This includes everything on earth and beyond; plants, animals, things, stars, everything you can imagine. I don't tend to focus on structured religion with its many rules. I don't believe God judges us and we should feel bad about ourselves. This creates the negative voice inside us and separates us from loving ourselves. Spirituality is much more than organized Religion. For me, whatever words you choose to use are your business; for me it is a Spiritual Energy that is the basis of all life and beyond. It is the unknown, the wonder that can't be "proven" so to speak.

I remember one time my son asking for our whole family to be the "same" religion. He knew I was raised in a different church than my husband. I decided that if that was important to him, I would make that happen. I decided to convert. I remember being nervous to tell my parents. *Would they be angry with me? Would they understand that to me, it didn't matter what organized religion that my family attended as long as I was able to raise my kids believing in God?* When I told my parents, my Dad responded, "Well, I think we are all talking to the same person." *He got it. Now, if you are wondering what religion I am, I will ask you, does it matter?*

"As you learn about your energy on a soul level, you will encounter topics and information that feel right to you as a core spiritual truth and some ideas that don't make any sense at all." ~ Melissa Alvarez

My Grandmother (my father's mother) and I on my wedding day.

Take what you want and leave the rest. For me, the dimes spoke to me, a true message from my Father, helping me understand that God is within me.

From a very young age, I always felt the presence of God. It is difficult to describe; other than, I know that someone somewhere cares about me and everyone else on Earth. It isn't like one ultimate power, it's more like all the people in Heaven loving me. I feel it in my gut and my heart. I first felt this in church when I was young. My Grandmother (my father's mother) was close to God. She read the Bible everyday, wrote in her journal and only said nice things about people. Never would you hear her say anything bad about anyone. My husband's mother is very similar in this way and has taught me a lot about being grateful for everything in my life. I loved sitting next to Grandma in church; I knew she got it. I could *feel* it. For me, being in church made me feel safe. I loved singing songs and learning in Sunday School. I felt a presence that I couldn't explain. My heart beat better when I was at church. For me, it wasn't about the people in the church, it was what I felt inside. I knew that God was speaking to me. He was helping me in a family that I didn't understand. When I was young, I envisioned everyone together believing in the same thing that I believed.

The moment in time that I felt the most connected to God and my Grandmother was when she and I found about a dozen four-leaf clovers at our family camp on Lake Elmore. It was a sunny day and my Grandmother and I were sitting near the sandbox next to the lake. She found the first one and showed it to me. I couldn't believe it! I wanted to be like her so I started looking for another one. We kept finding more and more. It was magical. I had never even seen one four leaf clover, but we found a dozen. We took them inside the camp and put them in a book so they would dry and I would be able to save them. When I think of that afternoon, I can see the sun shining on my Gram's face and hear her laughing. She is my angel. *When I find four leaf clovers now, could they possibly be a message from my Gram, saying hello? I believe so.*

As a mother, it was always important to me to pass the belief in God on to my own children. I knew there would be times in their lives when they would need to turn to Him to ask for help. Life can knock you down and it's important to know how to pray for guidance. My kids believed in God long before the dimes. Although I brought my kids to church often, for us, God was more than attending church. God was there for you always and forever.

One of the more positive memories that I have growing up was going to see the group of performers called, "Up With People". Wow. Talk about energy. During their songs and performances, it felt like a tsunami of love crashing on the entire audience. I soaked up all of the positive energy from those performances and dreamed of one day being on stage performing with this group. It was like God was in the room with all of us. The excitement, the energy, the positivity- I absorbed the energy into my body like I was a sponge soaking up water. I felt amazing after attending one of these shows. Their motto is,

"In our ever-changing global world, hope is the foundation for uniting people and communities. This is the heart of Up With People."

I have no idea how this particular show was in our community back then, but it was. Now, their shows aren't even close to Vermont. If only I could attend one of these, and take a hike once a week, I would feel so much better!

Does it matter what others think? My anxiety goes up as I share about my beliefs in God. Being vulnerable is not my thing. I like people to think

I have my life together. Well, Brene Brown sure did introduce me to being vulnerable, but writing this book feels like too much vulnerability.

"Daring Greatly means the courage to be vulnerable. It means to show up and be seen. To ask for what you need. To talk about how you're feeling. To have the hard conversations."~ Brene Brown.

I did not know how to even begin to do this. I keep writing even though I wonder...Should I be telling everyone all of this? Should I keep it to myself? What will my colleagues think? My past students? But the dime is the key. It helps me keep writing.

"When life calls us, that's when you have to answer," Louise Hay's voice echoes in my head.

Was I being called to do something? How would I know if this is what I was meant to do all along? A lot of people say that everything happens for a reason and the timing is always the way it is supposed to be. Was this true for me now? Was the timing exactly as it was planned?

There are many points in my life where I "checked out" and have no memory at all. During my teenage years, I would cry to a minister or guidance counselor; only to build my wall back up directly after letting them see my pain. I had no idea what the word vulnerable meant but I wasn't going to seem weak to anyone. I was unable to know how to deal with my feelings and had nobody to talk to. I was afraid that people might hurt me so I put up a wall to protect myself. It was like armor I put around my heart so I wouldn't get hurt. When I "check out" of my body, it is like I'm not present. My head is busy thinking about other things. It's like I time travel in my head. *How do I explain this to other people? I seem to spend so much time in my head instead of being present. Nobody will ever understand.*

I do remember one time when I was about 10 years old. I can recall some friends at school talking about doing something nice for their mother for Mother's Day. I decided I was going to get up early Sunday morning and make my mother breakfast in bed. I was so excited and thought it was such a fantastic idea. I was sure my mother would be so happy and proud of me for doing something nice for her. So, I proceeded to get out of bed around 7:00 that morning and went to the kitchen to start cooking some eggs. My mother heard me and came out to see what I was doing. I explained to her what I was doing and that I wanted to surprise her. She scolded me and told me to get back to bed this instant. It was "too early", she explained. I went back to bed, so disappointed. *How could she ruin my surprise? I thought I was doing something nice for her and she still spoke to me and made me feel horrible.* I remember lying in bed so mad that I couldn't get back to sleep. Then, about a half hour later, I get up out of bed. She comes out of the bedroom and tells me I can make her breakfast now. I refused. She had ruined it and I couldn't understand why she had done that. *My boys might sometimes wonder why I always appreciate everything they ever do for me. It's because of this story. When I tried to do something nice, I was not given the chance to show my mother love. I felt rejected and didn't know how to recover. I held that anger in my body for years.*

I remember another time when I was about 14 or 15. Well, I should say, I only remember the beginning. It was the first time I got drunk and don't really remember most of what happened. It was my cousin's wedding. One of my cousins or relatives started giving me drinks. They gave me rum and coke because it looked like I was drinking a regular coke. *Nobody would know that I had an alcoholic drink. I had never even tasted any alcohol before. I drank it like I drank a regular coke. I have no idea how many I drank and I have no* recollection of the rest of the night. *I know I didn't pass out. I have little*

blips of memories here and there. Laughing with my cousin. Arguing with my mom. And, at some point, leaving the reception.

I had learned in Health class that alcohol is a downer or depressant. But when the alcohol first hit my system, I felt all warm and tingly inside. It felt like my body came alive and there was an electrical current running through my entire being. I didn't feel down at all and wondered why the health teacher had said alcohol was a downer. I had been looking for somewhere to fit in my whole life. It seemed like alcohol helped me feel a sense of belonging. I felt connected to everyone who was drinking. But, ultimately this was a facade that clearly ended the next day. It was only a superficial feeling of fitting in.

I have always wondered if I did something embarrassing that night. My mom and dad never talked about it with me. Ever. They obviously knew I was drunk. They had to. Why wouldn't they talk to me about drinking alcohol? As a young person who didn't ever drink much, my first time drinking would most definitely have an impact on my future

This ability to build a wall would be my protection when I was afraid to let anything or anyone come in or out. I stuffed all of my feelings and didn't like to talk to people about some of what was happening inside me. At many times, I didn't always love myself, something that Anita says is key to being able to live like there is Heaven on Earth.

"The only thing you need to learn is that you already are what you're seeking to attain. Just express your uniqueness fearlessly, with abandon! That's why you're made the way you are, and that's why you're here in the physical world." ~Anita Moorjani

Anita received these messages from God during her Near Death Experience (NDE). Loving myself sounds so easy, yet is so difficult for me. I've always wanted to believe in myself and know that God is within me. I wondered how I would ever face my fear of loving myself. If God loved me, why couldn't I?

Recently a childhood friend of mine told me that he believes in signs from Heaven. This was, of course, after I shared about finding the dimes I believed to be from my father. He proceeded to tell me about a photograph being magnified so much that you could see a face inside an orb (a ball of light in a picture). *Were people starting to believe in this stuff? Were those floating lights outside my childhood room people? souls? Could my father really have placed those dimes in those exact spots? How could he do it without a physical body to set them there?*

"One of the newest ways in which angels are showing themselves to us is by appearing in photographs as orbs of light...The method works best when you hold the intention of seeing the angels while you're taking the photos." ~Doreen Virtue

While writing my dime story, I am on vacation with my husband in Florida. I decided to start writing as a way to try to heal my emotions. As I sit here on the beach writing this, my husband asks me what I am writing about. I answer, "Well, eventually it will turn into my dime story." He responds, "Are you writing a book?" I pause and say, "Maybe..." I get up to get a drink, thinking- what if he or someone doesn't like my book or doesn't understand any of it? My mother warned me never to write any-thing that would be embarrassing if someone saw it. My fear grips me. My gut actually hurts. Please- I pray- leave me to get lost in my writing so that I may find myself.

"How much we know and understand ourselves is critically im-portant, but there is something that is even more essential to living a Wholehearted life: loving ourselves." ~Brene Brown

Chapter 2 Meeting Jesus

"The fundamental message behind every NDE is one of love, peace and compassion for others; their transformational power transcends cultures, faiths and creeds. It is a message we can all benefit from without having to come close to death."~Dr. Penny Sartori and Kelly Walsh

While writing this story, I am dealing with, yet again, another pain in my root chakra. The pain was different than my back surgery twenty years ago but it felt like the message my body was trying to give to me was the same. I've heard over the years that writing can be therapeutic. But, I also remember my mother's warnings not to share too much of myself with others. I decide to take this week, while on vacation to begin writing my dime story. Anita Moorjani says we have to heal from the inside out- we have to deal with our feelings before we can physically heal. I think what she means is that in order to heal, we have to feel God's love within us. God is the only one who can truly heal us, but we have to believe in the process and change our negative thoughts to positive thoughts. We need to pray for ourselves and through the power of prayer, we will be healed. We have to learn to accept ourselves as God made us. Anita's father and Soni, both of whom had died, communicated to her during her NDE,

"Now that you know the truth of who you really are, go back and live your life fearlessly!"

I wonder how to do that after having ignored my feelings for so long? I remember one time trying to use cream on my psoriasis and a friend laughed at me, saying, "You're trying to heal it from the outside, not the inside." At the time that made no sense to me. I had no idea how to even begin to heal from the inside. *I had built a wall so strong, I couldn't even begin to tear it down. Now was the time to begin. I knew it would be the only thing that could heal me.*

It seems that sometimes our blessings have to come through pain. Through pain, we feel God nearby to help us through our trials.

Was the pain in my body and the trials I have been through actually blessings and messages from God? What if being born into my birth family was a time for me to grow? Would I be the same person if I hadn't had those experiences? Does it take everyone this long to figure out how to love oneself? Am I the only one who has a negative voice inside my head, speaking to me telling me everything that I have done wrong; ruminating on every little thing? I feel like I have two voices inside my head- one who is extremely critical and another that comes from someplace else. The one who speaks to me about following my dreams; or sending me random messages. Is this my intuition? Where do these messages come from? I knew I needed to listen to the voice who cheered me on, not the voice who doubted everything I had ever done in my life.

"Self doubt undermines the process of finding our gifts and sharing them with the world. Moreover, if developing and sharing our gifts is how we honor spirit and connect with God, self doubt is letting our fear undermine our faith." ~Brene Brown

I remember reading Louise Hay's book, You Can Heal Your Life, years ago when I had surgery on my lower back. Louise quotes The Course in Miracles saying that,

"all dis-ease comes from a state of unforgiveness, and that whenever we are ill, we need to look around to see who it is that we need to forgive."

Do I need to forgive myself or someone else? How will forgiveness help my physical pain? Have I been holding on to resentment and anger? Was this, in turn, making me ill from the inside? Will my inner voice help me discover my emotions that will in turn heal my physical body? Will I be able to change my inner voice and listen to God more?

Now, here I sit thinking- this is dumb to think that anybody would be interested in my story. 'I'm not a writer- never will be,' my negative voice sings to me. I hadn't passed the writing exam years earlier in college and forever after I was scared to write. Right now, the thought of sharing this with someone scares the living crap out of me. I will be rejected yet again and I will be a failure, not only as a writer but as a person. They will find out that I am not perfect. I make stupid mistakes all the time. People won't understand. They will talk about me. They...They...they....

As I write this, I worry about what others will think of my beliefs and ideas. Many people see me as a public school teacher, one who should not be talking about these types of things. One time a parent even mentioned the fact that teachers shouldn't be allowed to wear cross necklaces....as he eyed the cross necklace around my neck. *Really? I thought. Should I not get married either?* Spirituality, energy based healing, speaking to the other side and such nonsense isn't what teachers should be like. Remember- there is a separation of church and state; any of this may be seen as trying to influence children into believing in things such as Spirit, God, or souls living forever. I continue to write, knowing that in the end, I need to share my story and I am more than a public school teacher or administrator. I know too, that I am able to show up to work and by seeing a bigger picture, use my talents and abilities to make a positive difference in the work that I do. I like to think about sprinkling love wherever I go. *Is it important that I believe what I am doing comes from God? Yes. Does it matter that others know it is from God? Unfortunately, yes, as some don't believe in such a thing. Maybe I am the messenger. I have to accept that some will never understand.*

At various times in my life, I felt more connected to God and those times have kept me here on earth, even when I wanted to be in Spirit. I wanted to leave earth my first year in college. That year in college was difficult. In high school I hadn't been allowed to do much on my own. I was now living in a dorm, trying to grow up and make new friends. This is pretty darn hard to do when I felt totally alone and different than everyone else. I had nobody to really talk to about anything. I didn't grow up close to my sisters and I didn't feel emotional support in my family for the things I was going through. During high school, I had a few close friends who were a few years younger than me. They were my lifeline and helped me so much. But in college I was removed from the high school scene and felt weird going back for help.

Nobody else seemed to have the problems I was having. Why did I struggle so much? Please God, help me understand.

"When written in Chinese the word 'crisis' is composed of two characters. One represents danger. The other represents opportunity." ~John F. Kennedy

I dulled my pain and tried to fit in by turning to alcohol and drugs during my first year of college. In elementary and high school, I had what I call "automatic" friends. My family knew several families whom we did lots of things with on the weekends. We went snowmobiling, skiing, ice skating and lots of other fun things. These people were my automatic family friends because our families were close. I didn't have to do anything to be their friend. I was a part of the group. The other set of "automatic" friends I had were at school. I went to a small high school and my classmates were all super nice. I played soccer, basketball and softball. Although I wasn't that good, being a part of a team helped me have a core group of friends. I never felt close to many of my peers, but I always felt like I had a lot of friends. When I went to college, I tried to play sports. I thought it would work the same. Join a team, have some friends. I wasn't a very good athlete in high school and I never should have been trying to play college sports. If I wasn't able to play competitively in high school, it wasn't going to happen in college either. At the time, I had no understanding of this. I know it probably sounds dumb but never did someone say to me,(or did I think it myself!) "hey, you sat the bench mostly in high school, maybe college sports isn't for you." *I had no idea what to do with my time. Sports was how I spent my time and that was where I got friends so I thought that's what I should do.*

I soon felt like a failure and didn't know how to make friends. Instead, I turned to the crowd who drank and smoked weed, something I knew little about. I was trying to fit in somewhere.

Looking back, I'm not quite sure how I even got passing grades that year. I was lost but others thought I was fine. I am lucky that I lived through that first year. Often times during that year, I thought it would be better if I didn't have to live on earth. A voice inside my head would say, *"Just crank the steering wheel- hit that tree head on and then everything will be ok."* To this day, I don't know why I didn't do it, other than it wasn't my time. I think God had other plans for me. At the time it was difficult to believe that my life on earth was worth anything. Dr. Christian Northrup talks about jumping in front of a car in one of Louise Hay's videos. *I believe she understands. Someone so famous also thought it would be easier to leave this place. Wow... I didn't think famous people had negative thoughts like me. Especially Dr. Northrup- she is so positive!*

In college, I did find a few friends. I hadn't felt like I fit in anywhere my entire life. *Why would college be any different?* The biggest reason I felt like I didn't fit in during college was because I had missed the drinking age cut off. Right before I turned **18**, the law changed the drinking age from 18 to 21. That meant, since I was one of the youngest in my class (I started kindergarten when I was 4 instead of 5) and I had an October birthday, almost all of my peers were able to drink alcohol and go to bars. At that point, since I wasn't of age to drink, I wasn't allowed in bars. Now, I look back and most likely this saved my life. If I had easy access to alcohol at that time, most likely I would have OD'd on it (for those of you who were at the Van Halen concert in Montreal with me you know exactly what I mean when I write this.) I drank alcohol like water, just like my first drink of rum and coke. I had no idea how to pace my drinking so I drank way too much most of the time.

I used alcohol and marijuana to try to fit in, be cool and numb any feelings or emotions that I might have. *Why was I always so scared and unsure of myself? Everyone else seemed to have confidence. Why couldn't I?* One friend, in particular, invited me to her grandparents' house in Florida. Her grandparents would serve us alcohol by the pool. I felt so grown up. I didn't grow up around people drinking because of my Dad's heart attack when he was 46 years old. We would be sitting by the pool, and her grandparents would serve us beer in a frosted mug that had been in the freezer. For me, I had never experienced such a thing.

Alcohol and drugs made my anxiety and insecurities even worse. (I only smoked pot less than a dozen times, but I think it affected me way more than others.) Pot would make me nervous and paranoid. I only did it to try to fit in. Instead it increased that voice inside me; the one who criticized *everything* I did. I also didn't know when to stop. Because of this, I can barely remember some nights; especially one particular night at my friend's house. What I do remember of that particular night was meeting Jesus. *For real? a voice inside says. Who is ever going to believe that! Ha! Good luck with that one, my gut churns as I write. I remember listening to the soothing sound of Anita's Indian voice describing her near death experience in her audiobook, Dying to be Me. I think she will believe.*

I didn't believe it that night and have never told anyone about it until now. Many drinks later, I ended up in a spare bedroom, somewhere in my friend's house. Excited to be away from home, I was thrilled to meet her friends; hoping they would like me. Drinking gin and tonics, I was quickly drunk and passed out; well, sort of. My friend liked to smoke weed and laugh at everyone. Me, I barely even knew what weed was until I got to college. She loved to joke and laugh at things that people did- which didn't help my insecurities.

Somehow I ended up on the bed, where I passed out and rolled onto the floor. My eyes were closed but I could still hear the party. All I could hear was a sea of laughter. Everyone was laughing at me. My face was about an inch from the wall. I could have easily puckered my lips and kissed the wall. With a wave of fear gripping me, I wasn't inside my body anymore. I was floating above it and can see my body lying there on the floor. I remember hearing the buzz of the party, the music and seeing everyone in the kitchen laughing and enjoying the party.

That is when I met and talked with Jesus. Jesus was there to tell me it was ok. I was told that I had more time and to return to my body. I explained to Jesus that I did not want to return. This is what I dreamed of when I wanted to run into the tree. I wanted to stay in whatever place this was. It was easier here. I didn't think I would ever feel this comfortable. I don't remember much else, other than everyone laughing at me, as I was curled up in a ball on the floor next to the wall. I remember hearing my friend saying, "Look- she is so passed out!" *My worst fear coming true- laughing and making fun of me. I was frozen and couldn't respond. I did not have any control over my body. I couldn't move and I couldn't talk. I wondered if I would ever feel comfortable in my skin after this. Then everything went black.*

At the time, I thought it was a dream. *But, it felt so real. Was it a dream or was it a near death experience? Had the drugs and alcohol created a situation where my heart stopped for a few brief moments? Was this what Heaven was like? Whatever it was, I felt like it was a message from God. It felt real.*

I woke up the next morning in the same spot where I had passed out the night before. I was more at peace, not worried about approval from my friend. *What happened, I thought? Why was I so peaceful around these people? Usually I was a pile of nerves. Why didn't I feel that I needed to please them?* Everyone was laughing, asking how I was. I played along and never dared to tell anyone what happened. Heck- How could I?

I would be even more humiliated. I had met Jesus, even if I thought nobody would believe me and they would all think I was crazy. *I had no idea at the time what to do with this information, but, inside, I knew I had spoken with Jesus and connected to the place I dreamed about.*

On my way home from Florida that year I got a ride home with Eldon and Joyce Towle, the family who helped us with maple sugaring. Their son and daughter lived near Boston, so they picked me up from the Boston airport. Their son was ill with cancer. I knew he was in the hospital but had no idea how sick he was. Yet again, my mother hadn't shared with me the details. Similar to my father, "feeling ill" instead of having a heart attack that almost killed him, I was told, "Their son is getting help in the hospital for his cancer." Back then, cancer wasn't as prevalent and I had no idea that it could kill a person.

I remember going to see him in the hospital. His son was about 2 years old at the time and he jumped right up into the hospital bed with his father. I had never seen a sick person who I knew personally like this before. He was lifeless. He didn't respond to his family. *What is going on here? I didn't know he was this sick. What are the doctors doing to help him? I wanted to run. Seeing him made it a reality and I didn't know how to deal with my feelings. I was scared.*

For some reason, I remember everyone else leaving the hospital room. I was alone in the room with him. I walked over to his bed, touched his hand and then bounced back away from him like a magnet repelling against the opposite ends. I remember his eyes. I saw death and I knew that he knew that I saw it. I wanted the others to be around so that I wouldn't feel this. I didn't want him to know that I saw him transitioning to spirit. It didn't even seem like he was in his body. *I had no way of dealing with this information at the time and looking back to that moment, I know that God was in the room with us. I believe God was taking him out of his physical body to embrace him so that he wasn't in pain anymore. But, for me, a confused 18 year old, I had no way to express any of this. For others, it was normal to see him like this. For me, I would be confused until I read many books helping me understand death and dying. He died the very next day, after my visit. I thought it was my fault. I thought he had seen death in my eyes and gave up.*

As I write this, my husband went swimming in the ocean and then asked me what I was writing, "anything about us?" What I think he meant was "anything embarrassing?" I explain that writing this is therapeutic and that I need to do this in order to heal my pain. After reassuring him that I am not writing anything embarrassing (at least not for him!), he responds, "Whatever helps you and makes you feel better." This is another reminder that God brought him to me soon after the night I met Jesus. I am so very thankful for the way my husband loves me and accepts me. He understands and accepts that I have a connection to God and that it is important to me. Will he still love me when he reads this? 'Yes,' a voice whispers, 'of course he will.'

I ask him if he wants me to read some to prove there is nothing embarrassing for him. He says, "No, you can share it with me when you are ready." A feeling of acceptance for who I am washes over my entire being. I thank God that we were brought together right after my first year of college. If I hadn't gone to the movies that night and met him, I'm not sure I would still be alive.

Many years later, God helped me get sober and I am happy to say that I haven't had an alcoholic drink in about 20 years. And, I never smoked weed again after I met my husband. For me, it is a black and white decision- absolutely no gray area. I don't drink or smoke and that is all there is to it. I don't need to alter my body to enjoy life. I used to think that confidence came from a bottle, now I'm trying to find confidence inside myself.

When I look, I see Him everywhere. While I write this book....did I say book? No way, anxiety and fear grip me as I wonder if this will ever turn into a book. I'm not important like Brian Weiss, Anita Moorjani, or Wayne Dyer. I remember my Mother telling me about Wayne Dyer once. Of course, I knew way more than my mother and anything she likes, I will not like. This was years before I would discover Wayne and be forever influenced by his positivity. Does my story reveal any important messages? Will people think it is very exciting?

I think of the people I have shared my dime story with, including a writing teacher who encouraged me to write about it. I tried and struggled; there was so much more to tell than "just a dime". How could I share everything with everyone? They might not believe me. They might criticize me. They might make fun of me or my family. But, how could I not share the story? The positives had to outway the negatives.

"In order to succeed at being yourself, build confidence, and overcome insecurity you must focus on potential instead of limitations. In other words, focus on your strengths instead of your weaknesses." ~ Joyce Meyer

When I moved back home in May, after my first year of college, I noticed the energy of the plants and trees around me. Springtime in Vermont is an amazing rebirth after a harsh winter. That year, I felt the plants and trees welcoming me home. Clearing out my body from the booze and drugs that year, I began to see life a little clearer. I felt the spring breeze and smelled the flowers for the first time in a long time.

Graduating from Johnson State College!

MONICA L. MORRISSEY

-

Chapter 3   Faith

"For we live by faith, not by sight" 2 Corinthians 5:7
Believe what you do not see and see the possibility in all things.
I always wanted to believe in signs from Heaven. Some people talked about a rainbow being a sign from their Grandmother, a butterfly a sign from their mother. I hadn't really been taught that it was ok to believe in those things. Life tested my faith and my belief in everything. I have a sign in my house that says, *"**THIS HOME BELIEVES**"* To me, if I could teach my kids one thing- it would be this. Believe in Heaven. Believe in the signs. Believe in the unknown. Believe in a bigger purpose. Believe in miracles. Believe that there is good in the world. Believe in yourself. Believe that I am always with you. **Just Believe.**
"More than the other Divine guidance styles, claircognizants tend to waver when it comes to faith. When you're a thinker, it's easy to think yourself into a box of skepticism. Faith seems illogical and rests upon so many intangible factors." ~Doreen Virtue

I see God/Spirit everywhere. There is music playing as I eat my lunch on the patio of the condo. The ocean waves roll in and people splash in the pool. Coming from somewhere above me, the radio blares Christian music about feeling lonely in this world and God helping us through it.

I listen and know that it is a sign to continue to share my story. I listen to this song all the time. I can sing it by memory. I pay the Sirius radio premium each year so that I can listen to The Message every single day. I tried to live without it for a week and I hated it. Hearing this song playing now is a little unusual...*people at a condo in Florida playing Christian music? If I didn't have Sirius radio, I wouldn't know the song...interesting coincidence. Will there be more?*

I watch a bird creep around the corner of the fence. Our small condo deck is on the ground level; the bird about twenty feet away from me. He seems to think he belongs and makes his way around the corner of the building. Standing about **3** feet tall, he cranks his neck to look for something, maybe some food? Each step he takes, he looks around, shakes his feathers and continues his journey. *I wonder what message I can learn from him. It isn't important what I think of this bird. It's his story, not mine. Why should I judge him for not fitting in. Why is that important? Doesn't everyone want to feel like they belong somewhere? I know I do. For now, I remember that although sometimes I might not feel like I belong, it is fine to walk in that path; to not let fear or the belief that I don't fit in hold me back. The bird flies away and I wonder where life will take him next.*

I used to think poetry, messages, songs, etc. were dumb; especially things that couldn't be proven. Only for   *As I write the word dreamers, my pen runs out of ink and there is only the outline of letters, with no ink. Like a message so clear yet hidden. That specific word. Dreamers. The word dreamers looks like a ghost on paper. No ink, just a shadow of letters on the paper.* Speaking of dreamers and messages from God, was that a sign or do I ignore it? My brain trained for so long to not believe in foolish things, that it is difficult to believe in all the messages I encounter. *Am I a dreamer thinking anyone will want to read my dime story? Will it matter? I always doubt messages, but when people hear my dime story- everyone believes my father is sending messages from Heaven. Most people get goosebumps.*

One of the books I picked up at the bookstore on the way to the airport has some interesting things to think about. Brian Weiss helps me process where I am at right now.

"So many of our fears are based in the past, not the future. Often the things we fear the most have already happened either in childhood or in a past life. Because we have forgotten or only dimly remember, we fear that the traumatic event may become real in our future." ~ Brian Weiss

The words help me feel safe in the present moment. I know that my fear is from the past.

"If you are ruminating about the past or worrying about the future, you will completely miss the experience of enjoying the cup of tea. You will look down at the cup and the tea will be gone. Life is like that. If you are not fully in the present, you will look around and it will be gone. You will have missed the feel, the aroma, the delicacy and beauty of life. It will seem to be speeding past you.

The past is finished. Learn from it and let it go. The future is not even here yet. Plan for it, but do not waste your time worrying about it. Worrying is worthless. When you stop ruminating about what has already happened, then you will be in the present moment. Then you will begin to experience joy in life." ~Brian Weiss

This message speaks to my core being, my root chakra and my breath. A voice speaks, "Breathe every time you worry or want to be present." This helps me enjoy Florida, every moment I make a connection or feel my pen hit the page.

When I was writing this morning a neighbor posted a song on Facebook. The song was about wanting to be different. This is another song that I listen to all the time- I envision myself living differently, the way I was born to live. The way my soul wants so desperately to live.

I cried when I listened to the video. The song reminds me of two of my nephews. Tyler, who died suddenly in a car crash and Micah, his brother. The sudden death of Tyler is when I started learning about souls, spirit energies and connecting with people in Heaven. Soon after his death, a colleague introduced me to Brian Weiss. Brian Weiss was a skeptic. He was an atheist and a scientist. Then his first patient, Katherine, began opening a new idea to him. While Dr. Weiss had her under hypnosis, she remembered several traumas. She told him about things that happened to her in a previous life. When she came back the next week, her phobia was gone. It was like it had disappeared after the hypnosis. She had a fear of water. Poof- gone! *Could past life regressions really help people? Is this why some people have extreme phobias? Are they carrying it in their soul lifetime after lifetime? Am I holding pains in my body from another lifetime?*

Through losing Tyler, my family and I had to pray to help each other get through that time. I always say it is normal for a person to lose their parents. It's part of the way the world works. *But I don't think a parent should have to bury their child.*

If we are willing to listen, I believe God will speak to us in ways we might have missed otherwise. *Tyler still speaks to me.*

As I think about my fear of facing who I am and trying to let my positive energy guide me another Christian song plays from somewhere above me. It is a song about fear. It is a very clear message to me that in order to listen to my soul's calling, I need to overcome my fear. I need to listen to my faith instead.

A voice inside me says, "It's ok. Face your fear. You have support now and you know that Spirit is everywhere, helping you forgive and accept yourself." Why are all of these spiritual songs playing right at this moment in time? Never before did I hear this type of music playing in a public place. Or, maybe the signs were there but I wasn't listening. I was too caught up in life and society so I never noticed the signs. Maybe I was spending too much time listening to my ego, judging others instead of listening to Divine guidance that was there all along. Had I spent my life being busy- all the time in my head instead of being in the present moment? Would I be able to slow down and connect with Spirit? Would learning to be still help me connect to the "something else", I had always felt inside? Listen, I think. Have Faith, I think.

Wait, is Faith like the wind? The wind blows but one cannot see it. We all know the wind is there because of the effects it has on other things, like leaves and flags. You know it is windy by looking outside and seeing all of the leaves blowing on the trees. Is Faith like that?  *When I share my dime story, people get goosebumps. Are they feeling faith blow onto them like the wind hitting their skin? Will writing this story help spread Faith throughout the world? Listen to the wind. It has the answers.*

"When angels or deceased loved ones come extra close, you can feel their presence. Many people I interview can recall when they sensed specific spirit nearby. Most say something such as, 'Yes, I could feel my mother with me the other night. It seemed so real, but I still wonder if I was just imagining it.'"~Doreen Virtue

Chapter 4 My Experiences with Death and connecting with Spirits

"The word angel means 'messenger'. Angels bring messages from the Divine Mind of our Creator." ~Doreen Virtue.

"We are always loved. We are never alone." ~Brian Weiss

I wasn't allowed to have pets growing up because I think my parents were worried that the pets would die and I might cry. I didn't attend many funerals before the age of 18. When I was 18, I went to a funeral for an older neighbor on the lake. I went alone and, much to my surprise, it was open casket. I didn't even know they did that. I was shocked to walk in and see the physical body. I felt a presence when I walked in but I was too shocked to even understand what was happening and had no knowledge about connecting with souls who had transitioned back to Spirit energy. Now I have a whole new definition of what death means.

Sometimes spirits give me messages in my dreams. Recently, a high school friend's father came to me in a dream. He said, "would you please let them (his family) know that I am really sending all of those messages. They don't believe in these messages." In the dream, it was exactly his face as I remember him. During the dream, he had looked deep into my eyes to make sure I received the message and would deliver it. Of course, this was after I had found THE dime, the key to me believing that I knew my father was connecting with me. My friend's father knew that I had to believe now and he wanted me to get the message to his family. My father and he were friends so it would make sense that they were sharing this new spirit communication system. When I messaged my friend, she was in tears and thanked me for the message. I have no idea what the messages were, but she said the timing of my message was so meaningful. *Synchronicities, like the friend posting the song on Facebook. Are they planned by someone else?*

My insecurities tell me I'm not really a medium or anything so don't bother thinking I am anything special. My anxiety goes up because I'm afraid people will think I am crazy and not understand what I am talking about. My family sometimes picks on me. I even say it myself actually! They call the healing, reading and work I do on myself, "voo-doo work". It's said with love, as they don't always understand what I am doing. But, at times, it gives me high anxiety because I am worried what others will think of me. What a lot of people don't realize is that I have read so much about soul work and connecting with Spirit, that for me it is the way the universe works. Everyone should know about this. I begin to wonder if all of the books I have read have actually taken the information from the Bible and translated it without an organized religion's focus tied to their name? What if everyone believed in the same things about God/Spirit and didn't have different churches? Would we all be allowed to share our beliefs?

Earlier this year I shared parts of my dime story with a colleague. I remember Michelle looking right into my eyes when she said, "You are an empath." *I thought, what? What does she mean? What is an empath? I don't really want to tell her that I don't know what she is talking about. Is that like a medium? I've been to mediums before but I don't think I hear messages from dead people in my head....or do I? What's the difference between an empath and a medium? I think about the mediums I have been to. They can "hear" messages "from Heaven" at any given moment. How do mediums know their thoughts are coming from Spirit, like the Spirit communication I had so clearly explained to my father? Isn't what we hear in our head our own thoughts? How do I distinguish my own thoughts from a message? And, if I am an empath, what exactly does that mean? Will people accept me if I am an empath? What will my family and friends think? I guess it won't matter because I don't think I can change who I am. I mean I am who I am, right? It's not like I have a choice.*

When I say spirits, I'm not talking ghosts, like the movies. I'm talking about an energy, a presence, a knowing. Something one can "sense" or a sign that reminds us of someone who has journeyed on. The kind of feeling that one has to have *faith* in order to believe it to be true. It's like the feeling of the wind on your skin; you can't see it, but you know it is there.

One of the first times I felt consciously connected to a spirit who was a relative was my Grandmother (my mother's mother). At the time, I was 21 years old, had no understanding of spirits and nobody to talk about my feelings. Most likely my Grandmother had an aneurysm or a stroke. I'm still not exactly sure which it was that caused her to decline so rapidly. My parents didn't share information with me about her condition- only that she was in the hospital. This was like when my father was in the hospital for the first time. I was about 13 years old and I was a candy striper at the hospital. I remember walking down the hallway with Dr. Blowers, a friend of my dad's. Dr. Blowers says, "Well, your father was lucky to survive such a massive heart attack. It will be a long road to recovery, but he can do it." Wait, *what? My father had a heart attack? My mother had only said, "Dad wasn't feeling well so he went to the hospital." Dr. Blowers had no idea that I wasn't told about my father's condition.* The same would be true when my Grandmother was in the hospital. I wouldn't be told any information- other than she wasn't 'acting right.'

I remember arriving at the hospital to see my parents standing in the room, away from my Grandmother's bed. I went right to her bedside, holding her hand, speaking to her; telling her how much I loved her. At the time, it was as if I was drawn to her like a magnet. But this time, instead of repelling, I was pulled towards my Grandmother. Even though she looked like she was sleeping, I know she was listening to me. When I spoke, she squeezed my hand and I know for certain that she heard me. *At her bedside* I felt my Grandfather standing right there with us. It isn't like I actually see his physical body. It is a sensation of energy, a moment in time where I feel the love of spirit through my Grandfather, someone who passed shortly before I was born. I didn't necessarily know it when it was happening, but as I write about it and think back to that moment in time when I was holding my Grandmother's hand, I can feel him there with us. Without proof, I never dared to trust my intuition. *What would people think if I thought that my Grandfather was there in the room? Was he waiting for her? Was she aware that he was there and it was safe to leave her body? Many thoughts cross my mind. Is this what it means to be empathic? Doesn't empathic mean you show a lot of empathy? Kind of like sympathy, but different? My mind still wonders.*

After my Grandmother passed away in February, my husband asked me to marry him. In the middle of a winter storm, he brought me to "our" hill, where we had walked on our very first date. When we were dating, we spent many nights walking that very hill. Spending the rest of my life with him would be a dream come true. God had brought him to me and he would be my rock, always accepting and loving me as I am. My parents asked us if we wanted to buy my Grandmother's house. At the time, we thought it would be better than renting. While we cleaned out the house, I felt like my Grandmother was there 24/7, supervising the entire project. This was ok when all of the family was there but when I moved in with my new husband, *you can imagine my confusion.* My Grandmother was a very proper woman, who refused to smile for any pictures. I sensed her energy in every room as we made her house our new home.

Well, as you can imagine, I had a difficult time, as a newlywed, enjoying my life with my new husband, with a Grandmother who I thought was watching my *every* move.....both day and night. Because of my embarrassment, I would suppress my connection with spirit. If I look back at that time, I remember being so happy living in her house and feeling her all around me. I can still feel her as I write this and I can envision myself inside the house where she was watching over me, not in a weird way but in a protective, loving way- you know? *A spirit kind of way.*

"And don't worry that Grandpa is watching when you shower or make love. These souls aren't voyeurs. In fact, there's some evidence that spirit guides don't see our physical selves on Earth; they perceive our energy and light bodies instead. So they simply understand your true thoughts and feelings during each circumstance."
~Doreen Virtue

I don't really remember when spirits first started visiting me. It would happen in that in between sleep and wake state- not quite awake yet not quite sleeping either. I would push them away, almost reflexively, *as if I was scared.* One time I had an awful experience- I envisioned 1,000 skeletal looking spirits - all wanting my attention, and heckling me. I did not understand what was happening and again, had nobody to talk to. I don't believe in Hell, I believe everyone crosses over into the light. But I do think there are some low energy spirits who are very troubled and try to seek someone who might be able to help them. I told them to leave me alone because I was sleeping; something that my family can tell you is a problem now. I never want to be woken up- I hate it! I have a lot of sleep issues (both going to sleep and staying asleep) so when I am asleep, I want to stay asleep. I didn't want whoever these people were to disturb me. A part of me really wanted to help them all. But, alas, that would be impossible. *How is it possible to help so many troubled people? Instead, I try to sprinkle love wherever I go.* I have now requested that only positive spirits visit me and that only love and light are welcome in my home. I have put up a positive light to protect myself and have never had the experience that I had years ago.

Now I get bearhugs, a feeling of heaviness or a feeling like someone is sitting on the edge of the bed. I still have difficulty understanding and accepting these feelings. *Is this what she meant when she said I was an empath? I don't understand how this all works.* In this state, I have a weird feeling engulf my body. I am separated from my body and I cannot control it. When this happens, I literally can't move. I feel like I am trapped inside my body. I can't escape, even though I feel like I want to. I want to run or get up out of bed. But, in that in between state of wake and sleep, it is like I am paralyzed. The only thing that I can do is breathe. I am unable to move. *I think back to when I had my near death experience. What was happening? Is this my soul that is disconnecting from my body? How do I get back to my body so I can move? It is the most unusual sensation for sure.*

My Dad and I next to his business truck. I see Goodyear signs all the time!

I believe spirits can show in many different ways. Sometimes it is in a physical form and sometimes it is an energy; a feeling. The physical form comes in many different ways- For some, it is butterflies, dragonflies, sunflowers, or rainbows. For me personally, it is four leaf clovers from my Grandmother Palmer, dimes from my Father, pennies and rainbows from my Mother, GoodYear signs from my Father and Grandfather and the list keeps going on and on. (My father and grandfather sold GoodYear tires at the family business.) For me, it's real. It's not just cute and nice that I "think" that they are sending messages. *It really is them.* I know others who want to believe so much but doubt whether or not it could really happen. *When I begin sharing parts of the dime story, many people believe they are from my father. So many synchronicities happening all around me. I wonder if other people ever doubt their own beliefs? The conversations I had with my father before his death make the dimes so much more meaningful. Dad's spirit sending messages to me that I am not alone. The story of the dimes is so much more than the dimes. The entire story helps me understand and believe that our souls' journeys go on forever and ever.*

I have attended many more funerals over the years. I cried with my family at my nephew, Tyler's funeral. The most difficult part of funerals for me now is watching my own children in pain. Tyler was killed on impact in a car crash, the result of his side of the car hitting a brick mailbox. Through one of his best friend's, Red Sox pitcher David Price, Tyler is remembered. *As I write, I cannot stop crying as I feel Tyler's strong presence encouraging me to tell my story. I wonder, was Tyler like me? Does he want to help the world be a better place through my writing? I know the answer, yes. He says, "Aunt Monica, tell your story. It's important and I am one of the keys to your story." These messages sometimes are so strong that I wonder where they come from. When I listen AND feel, they are overwhelming. A poem by Tyler March 7, 2001*

His Road Not Taken
Going along the path,
There's a split in my way
Which way should I chose?
I will find out another day.
The two paths are different,
I don't know which one to choose.
One seems to be very new,
The other has been stomped on by shoes."

After Tyler's death would come unexpected lessons for me. I was introduced to Brian Weiss and the idea of past lives, a totally new and different way of thinking about life and souls. *Could going deep within the soul to remember a past-life really heal the pains from this life? Were souls really floating around waiting to enter a human body to work out their lessons? Brian Weiss was shocked when his first patient was healed from exploring another lifetime. He was a skeptic, but his patients showed him that by going deep within the soul to remember, they could heal past pain.*

"Yet these memories allowed her to recover from her recurring nightmares and anxiety attacks in a way she'd never experienced."
~*Brian Weiss.*

"The awareness that we have multiple lifetimes, separated by spiritual interludes on the other side, helps to dissolve the fear of death and bring more peace and joy into the present moment."~Brian Weiss

How would anyone else ever believe this? I wonder...

The year after Tyler's death, I would meet a medium for the first time to learn about what my life lessons were. She shared lessons that I needed to work on in this lifetime, all similar to other lifetimes prior to this one. I remember one of the first questions she ever asked me- "What do you do if you come to a tree or a rock in your path?" My answer- "go around it, climb over it, whatever I need to do to get to the other side!" She responded with another question, "How about taking a different path?" Oh- wow- that idea had seriously **never** crossed my mind! *I had no idea how to begin to take a different path. Was this book my new and shiny path? Would it help my soul discover a different way to live? Different than the way I was raised. Did I need to leave behind my childhood beliefs to create a new life- one filled with Divine Guidance on my new path?*

After I read Brian Weiss's books, I started reading Wayne Dyer's books. Wayne explains how important it is to find "one's true calling." He wrote The Shift and I literally felt my world shifting. So many other experiences help me begin to totally change my way of thinking about life. It was changing my brain. I had thought life was one thing, yet was slowly being introduced to many new ideas. Life was so much bigger than what I thought it was. I wasn't sure who to share these "New Age" ideas with. *People wouldn't understand, like I felt my mother didn't understand. People don't read as many books as I do.* Everyone is so busy with life. I thought people wouldn't believe me. *That is, until, the dimes started coming one by one. Then I would start sharing more and more, with anyone who had the time to listen. When I shared my story, people believed and even shared some of their stories with me. But, I never had time to tell the entire dime story. There was so much more to tell. How did this all fit in with all of these different ideas about souls, past life regressions, talking with people who had passed on.....How would I ever be able to explain this to others?*

Be in the now. Face my fears. Release old beliefs. Don't hold on to outdated thoughts. Ask God for help. Follow your dreams. Remember, your body is listening to everything you are thinking, a voice from within guides me as I write.

Tyler's friend, David Price believes that spirits are all around us. They were best friends all through high school and college.

"No one enjoyed David Price's performance in Tuesday night's All-Star Game as much as Tyler Morrissey did. He was in the upper deck. He was behind the dugout. He was behind the plate. He was even on the mound with Price. After all, as far as Price is concerned, he always is."~ *Gary Shelton St. Petersburg Times July 13, 2010.*

"Almost 3 months after Tyler's death, David felt Tyler's presence- helping David as he began his MLB career as a pitcher. This was something that Tyler always believed would happen to David and David knew that Tyler's spirit was right there with him every step of the way." ~ *Gary Shelton St. Petersburg Times July 13, 2010.*

Just watch Price when he pitches for the Red Sox or previous games with Tampa Bay. Does he ever look up towards Heaven? Or tap his heart?

-

5

Chapter 5 Before the Dimes

"We have so many more intuitive abilities that we know or use."
~Brian Weiss

"Information about our past lives and the spiritual dimensions can also be gleaned from other intuitive insights as well as from dreams, through meditation, or even spontaneously, as in deja vu experiences." ~Brian Weiss

The same year that Tyler died, 2008, my Mother almost died from congestive heart failure. She would be taken early in the morning in an ambulance to the hospital to find out that she needed open heart surgery to fix a valve in her heart. Later we found out that she hadn't been to the doctors in 33 years; the last time she went to a hospital was to give birth to her last child! My father had had open heart surgery three times, but she had never had surgery. She seemed to hate hospitals if she was the patient. She seemed fine if it was someone else.

I can remember the day right after her surgery. My mom was in an intensive care unit that included 2 patients and about 10 hospital staff. When my father and I walked in to see her, she was unresponsive. The tubes connected to her were helping her breathe. She was lifeless. I felt like she wasn't really there. The other patient in the room was a good distraction for both Dad and myself. Dad knew the guy. He joked around with my dad. Mom was heavily sedated and, although the jokes made Dad laugh, I'm sure he was struggling. It was easier for us to joke and talk than to really feel our feelings- scared to admit that we weren't sure if Mom was going to make it through this.

After our brief visit, we went to the waiting room. There we would meet the man's daughters. One of his daughters would come into my life later on to become the principal at the school where I taught 6th grade. This was an important time in my life as she basically kept me in the field of education; something that I had been thinking of leaving due to certain people in my career wanting to "get rid" of me. At the time, I doubted that I should even be in education and wondered what I should do with my life. I loved teaching all of my students but sometimes the politics of education can be a real downer. The woman I met in that waiting room would forever change the course of my life's journey. I would stay in education because of her encouragement. *Sometimes people don't know the effect they have on others. Did this woman know the difference she made in my life? Well, how would she ever know if I wasn't willing to admit this before?*

In the waiting room, introductions were made all around. This family knew my husband's family. Later, with the strain of the day, my sister-in-law took my father home. Soon, everyone else left too but I stayed a little longer. The small waiting room, located directly next to the doors of the intensive care unit, had changed from a busy, lively place full of friends and laughter to me sitting alone wondering about my mom. *As I sit here writing this, I feel goosebumps all over- a tingly sensation. Is this a sign of someone present helping me work through this- and write this book? Or sending me a sign that I wasn't truly alone in that waiting room after all? Does anyone else ever feel this type of 6th sense? How does one learn to believe in this stuff? What if someone laughs and says this is all hogwash? Will I always feel like I need to hide this part of me? Does this have something to do with being an empath? Why isn't there some sort of physical proof so that we actually see something? The dime....that was my physical proof, wasn't it? Weren't the goosebumps like the leaves on the trees? Was the feeling on my skin showing me that an energy was near?*

Within minutes of everyone leaving, the hospital staff started running through the doors of the ICU. One doctor looks at me as he goes through the doors. I see the fear in his eyes but am all alone with my worries. I know something is going on but am too scared to ask any questions. *Is it my mother or the other guy?* I sit quietly for what seems like a long time. A sudden stillness comes over me. I sit and wait. Finally, a doctor comes out to explain that Mom had "coded", meaning they had to "bring her back". I hear their words, yet it takes me a minute to digest the information. I feel dreamy, almost like I am hearing their words but can't really understand them. They ask me if I want to go in to see my Mom. I walk into the room to see Mom's body there, but she doesn't look like she is even alive. Without the distraction of my father, I see my Mother the way she is- empty. I almost run from the room. I think of the boy in the book Heaven is for Realby Todd Burpo and Lynn Vincent. In that book, the little boy was having surgery and almost died. He was able to see what was happening around the hospital during his surgery, like when I was watching the party even though my body was on the floor of the bedroom. *Did my Mom have any sort of out of body experience that she never spoke about? Did she know I was there? Was she still inside her body?* I leave the hospital lost and crying.

My mother did recover but she would need to go for another surgery years later to fix the valve again. Eventually she would try to eat better and ride her bike, but it would never be enough to battle heart disease. The doctors reported after her heart surgery that, at some point earlier in her life, she had a massive heart attack and only half of her heart was able to work properly. When the doctors suggested another surgery, Mom refused.

From that point on in my life, I began to take my parents to various doctors appointments. Although it was difficult to take time off from teaching, I felt it was important to spend time with and help my parents. It was difficult to be away from my own kids, who were in high school at the time. I know that I showed my kids how to take care of others by action, not words. When I lost both of my parents I remember my sons saying to me, "Mom, you sure are strong." *Believe me when I say, the only thing that got me through this time in my life was my faith and my belief in God. He helped me through it and I couldn't have done it without the support of my husband, my two sons and God.*

It's difficult to balance work, kids, ailing parents and have time to process all of the reading I was doing. At the time I began to work toward my Master's degree in education and I would not have the time to read anything for pleasure. My Mom was always difficult to deal with, and even more so when her health began to decline. But I accepted her for who she was and I have no regrets. I did my best to care for my parents. A medium gave me insight as to why my mother treated me the way she did. She suggested that Mom might be jealous of my connection with my father, *one that I feel went beyond this realm.* Once I saw that piece of the puzzle, it was clear that this had been impacting my relationship with my mother. I began to change the dynamic when I took care of my parents. I began doting on my Mom and asking her all sorts of questions; she loved to talk. My father actually glowed with happiness when I did this. It was amazing to see the change in both of them. This one little piece of the puzzle helped change our relationship during those last few years. Being able to see her point of view helped me understand our relationship. *But, when she was alive, wasn't able to connect with my father or my mother in the way that I wanted to.*

As I write this, I begin to wonder what my parents might think of this book. Are they with me now as I write?

This reminds me of being vulnerable, something I never really thought about until one of my professor's introduced it in one of my master's class. Thanks Jacqui! As part of learning how to be a good leader, she introduced us to the concept of vulnerability, or, basically, "being human"- not perfect. She introduced my class to Brene Brown. We watched her YouTube video about vulnerability. If you haven't seen it, go now and watch it! It will forever change your life. I began my understanding of being open to vulnerability. To me, it meant embarrassment. Things that I didn't want people to know about me. Things I wanted to hide from people so others wouldn't know that I wasn't perfect. Looking like the perfect family is what I had been taught. In my career, I had tried to be the perfect teacher. Now, those walls began to crumble. During this time, I felt that I had to be the strong one. *Sharing my story is going to make me vulnerable. This scares me so much. How will I ever get over this feeling so that others can hear my story? If I show vulnerability, will it help others?* In my Master's degree program I had to conduct an Action Research project in my classroom instead of writing a thesis. My entire project was about how making mistakes helps our brain to learn. This was ok for Math class, but I didn't want anyone to see my life mistakes. That would make me feel shame and embarrassment. I would be vulnerable, which was something that I didn't know how to do. I had to learn that some people would know and understand the love that I have. I know that whatever I do, if I do it with love, no matter how someone reacts, it would be ok. Being vulnerable was going to take a lot of courage.

I recall my work on Action Research for my Master's Degree. I was expected to read, understand and integrate several researchers. I didn't think I could do it, but my professor did. How does one integrate all of the research into one big project? I did it- Carol Dweck- growth mindset. Jo Boaler- growth mindset, brain research and teaching math. Etc. etc. I find as I write that I can compare my life to one big Action Research project too. I found things along the way that I learned and integrated into my life. Many different authors have planted many different seeds of knowledge. As I began to reflect on my journey, I realize all the authors who have guided me in my life. It was like Action Research for my soul's growth.

One of my main life lessons is to enjoy the journey, the ups and the downs. During Action Research and life, I wanted to finish all of my projects. At times, it was all so tiring. If I finished everything, then maybe I would be able to relax. Instead, I was like the energizer bunny- I would keep going and going. Having something completed made me feel like I accomplished something. *"Enjoy the journey,"* they suggested. *Did anyone know how difficult this was for me? I had to realize that life was about the journey, not the destination. Like Action Research for my Master's degree, I had been conducting my own research about life for years. So many teachers helped me understand that the work is worth it.*

As I worked towards my Master's degree, I took care of my parents during their last days on earth, and was still trying to raise my kids. I find it difficult to be in the present moment because I am always trying to finish everything before I can relax. I wanted everything to be completed. The estate, my degree, everything. I wanted to have some free time for me. I was taking care of everyone and studying all the time. I was so exhausted that it was difficult to function. My battery was empty. *As I write, I know I am also meant to share my stories to help others. I am not famous, but I have an interesting tale to tell.*

"Today is your life, Live with intention
Speak the Truth, Make mistakes
Take risks, Have an adventure
Embrace the Journey."
~Anonymous

Nowadays, sayings like this one are so common. People have these types of signs in their house, on Facebook, Instagram and everywhere. Growing up, these guiding quotes were never there for me. When shared they are a positive part of technology. I think about my journey in life. What have I learned? Have my experiences led me to believe certain things? Things that others will have no understanding because they haven't lived through my life? How can we all be more patient? How can we all help each other?

I remember another time sitting in the waiting room. This time I was with my mother while dad was having procedure done on his heart. I got a text message that my uncle, my mother's brother, had a heart attack and is on his way to the same exact hospital. *How do I tell my mother that while her husband is in surgery right now, her brother had a heart attack? I remember how long it took my father to heal from his first heart attack and I remember Dr. Blower's words, "He almost didn't survive."* I break the news to Mom and she takes a big inhale, covers her mouth and says, "That's how my father died."

Moments later, my uncle is wheeled in and stops to visit with us in the waiting room. *Can you believe it? They bring the patients right by where we are sitting in the waiting room? This is a huge hospital. I would think there might be a different hallway. Well, I guess it makes sense since we are in the wing where they do heart surgeries.*

My uncle was ok and later, he and my father try to convince the doctors that they should get a special price on their surgeries. Since they were family they thought it should be kind of like a buy one surgery get one free, like buying something at Price Chopper. Buy one heart surgery, get the other for free!

My Grandfather (my mother's father) died a few weeks before I was born. My mother had told me that it was difficult when I was born because he loved kids so much. Everyone knew that he would have loved another granddaughter. His name was Rudolph and I think how cool that name is. I wish I could have met him. I have no idea what that had been like for my mother. Had losing her father so young changed her? Did I actually not know my mother because I hadn't had her experiences in life? Had I been so busy judging her that I hadn't taken the time to learn what her life's journey had been like?

I'm thankful for the time spent with my Mom and Dad. I learned a lot about life and death during that time. Even though my mother didn't like to talk about personal things, my father and I talked a lot during our daily trips to the hospital to see my mother. During that time, I got a glimpse of some of their life stories. I began to understand that I knew little about their life experiences. *What made them who they were?*

Of course, the dimes from my Dad would teach me so much more.

-

Chapter 6 Messages and My Inner Voice

"This is very significant proof that our thoughts have powerful physical effects on our bodies and that we can't afford to ignore them." ~Dr. Christian Northrup (www.heartmath.org)

When I was first married, my husband asked me what I wanted for my birthday that year. I told him I would love a Mickey Mouse watch. I had been to Disney as a child and adult, and I had sung the song Mickey Mouse March as a child so much that I felt connected to that Disney character. I also loved the story of how Walt Disney got his start in creating his company. My husband went in search of a Mickey Mouse watch. Of course, this was long before Amazon Prime. He went to the local jewelry store and explained that he was looking for a watch for his wife. He was shown a few watches, mostly expensive. Then the clerk jokingly says, "Well, I do have this one Mickey Mouse watch." My husband's response? "Oh wow! That is **exactly** what I was looking for!" Perfect timing for the perfect watch.

As the pages flow, I am amazed at how therapeutic writing can be. My husband questions me again, 'What will people learn about me if and when people read this?' I share the part about him accepting me and how thankful I was to meet him at that particular time in my life. I begin to cry. I thank him for always accepting me for who I am. He asks me not to cry. I tell him I have been bottled up for years and need to let a lot of stuff go. This will help me in my healing. I begin to share some of my stories of other signs from above. He understands and leaves me to myself, allowing me time to write.

I often give other people advice. It comes naturally. I always want to help people. I have had so many different health issues over the years, it feels like I could help anyone figure out how to improve their health. I've also had so many events that have shaped my understanding about life- raising kids, losing my parents, executor of the estate, back surgery, getting sober. All of these things help me connect to stories from people going through hardships in their own lives.

I realize now that all of my advice that I have so freely given, is actually advice I should have given to myself. Most recently a woman, who has had difficulty carrying a baby to full term, confides in me. I tell her that I sense her great grandparents are with her and she needs to not only focus on the front of her abdomen, but also her back. During this trip, I realize that I also need to look at the possibility that my pain may be radiating from my back. I also feel like my Great Grandmother is around me, guiding me. Light bulbs! Fireworks! *I realize that all these years I was freely giving others advice, it was actually things that I needed to hear. I call this the Boomerang effect. I try to help others and it was actually the words that I needed to hear. Some people speak about projecting onto others what is going on internally with yourself. Boomerang. Right back at ya!*

I also wonder about the back metaphor. Did I need to look in the past (behind me) to find my answers? Would writing about this help me heal my past and help me move forward in my future? I had to believe that this was true.

I think of all the advice I have given recently. I tell new teachers to run, hike, make sure they take time to relax. I give Reiki to the teachers. I know that maybe if I went and got Reiki from someone, maybe I, too, could heal. Essential oils- I teach others about them and forget to use them myself. Emotional Freedom technique (EFT tapping)- I brag about how well it works for stress, but rarely use it myself. I told a Tracy's daughter, Chelsea, that she should write a book.... And now-here I am. *I find it easier to give advice than to receive it myself.*

I hear voices of all of the advice through the years- me telling others what I think might help them. Now, I see the voice was trying to talk to me. You see, I have an insatiable desire to try to help others. It's like I absorb their energy and want them to get well. It's difficult to explain but I love helping people. Even though I know many alternative ways to cure illnesses and heal, I don't use them on a regular basis. I might use them on vacation or in the summertime but they were not part of my normal routine. When teaching, I was "too busy" to do them. I liked to get to school early in the morning so there was no time for exercise or to prepare meals. After school, I had meetings or was too tired. So, out of 12 months during the year, I was only using these tools for about two months total. I tried to do these things only when I was on school vacations. It's difficult for me to balance work and take care of myself. *Instead of preaching about it, I needed to take my own advice for once. Boomerang. Right back at me.*

My husband and I take a walk on the beach. We are both lost in our own thoughts. We talk about life and the people in our life. Friendships, divorces, deaths. We think a lot of people we know most likely have in-securities. I say that I think at some level we all do, starting to admit my own insecurities. Admitting my insecurities would make me vulnerable, something I knew little about in my life growing up. So many messages coming to me as we walk and talk. I begin searching for dimes along the beach, wanting a sign to help me feel that I am walking my true path; something to give me the faith to believe. "That isn't how it works", a voice tells me. "You don't need physical proof. Faith is knowing He is there, even when you are unsure", the voice continues to explain. I stop looking for a dime. One will show up if and when it is the right time. I need to under-stand that the messages I am receiving while writing are from Spirit, not necessarily from my brain. Sort of like an internal guide inside me.

A baby girl in a bright pink hat waves to me as we walk. So precious and new, reminding me that souls come to Earth when they are ready. Some people believe that we choose our parents before arriving on earth. *Did I choose my parents in order to learn the lessons I needed to learn? What was I supposed to learn?* Babies have God within them. This is why it is such an amazing feeling holding a baby. I smile at her and continue walking and thinking.

I begin talking to my husband about all of the students I have had over the years. It wasn't about the great lessons in Math or Geography. It was me caring about each and every child. Remembering, that when each student was born, their family and friends went to the hospital to hold that new baby. They all deserved to be treated with love and kindness. I tried to learn about each student; making connections with them and discovering what they loved to do. I helped them be present in the classroom; creating a safe environment for them to learn. I encouraged them to share about whatever was worrying them and then focus on their learning. I always enjoyed helping students grow and learn. They all knew I cared. I knew about growth mindset long before Carol Dweck's research proved that positive thinking worked. I had to believe in these kids. Carol Dweck calls it growth mindset, but I call it Faith.

We plan and God laughs. Oftentimes, people use this phrase. For dinner that night, my husband and I can't decide. Do we want to eat outside or inside? We go back and forth. When we arrive at the restaurant, the hostess says we have an outside table right now or an inside one in about a half hour. "Ha!" I say to my husband, "We thought we had a choice when we really didn't. God decided where we should be- not us!" We both laugh on our way outside for dinner.

Teaching has been my entire life and, for most people who know me, that is all they really see. What if I decide to share this book with someone and decide I want to write about God and teaching? Will I be judged as a public school teacher? One who believes in God and weird things about souls returning to earth to grow and learn. Who knows? I think of the many doctors who were scared to share their beliefs, especially with their colleagues in the medical world. People like Brian Weiss, Judith Orloff and Christian Northrup. I am an educator who worries what other educators will think. My insecurities flare up right along with my physical pain. I continue to write. Brian Weiss says,

"Are you afraid of your reputation, afraid of what others think? These fears are conditioned from childhood or before."

Right, my fears do come from a childhood of feeling insecure.

"Love dissolves fear." ~Brian Weiss

Songs about fear play over and over in my head.

I remember Wayne Dyer commenting on something about spiritual beings...

"You aren't your work, your accomplishments, your possessions, your home, your family... your anything. You're a creation of your Source, dressed in a physical human body intended to experience and enjoy life on Earth." ~Wayne Dyer

I describe to my husband my hot flashes, another part of my life that is changing the way I live. "I don't know how to dress anymore," I explain. What I am really trying to say is, "I don't know how to move forward in my life- to live differently." See, I have been in both emotional and physical pain for years. I cannot ignore it any longer. I explain to my husband that during a hot flash I have to have a lot of patience, basically stopping time and making me fully present in the moment. Hot flashes are forcing me to be present in the moment.

"Research into the physiological changes taking place in the perimenopausal woman is revealing that, in addition to the hormonal shift that means an end to childbearing, our bodies- and, specifically, our nervous systems- are being, quite literally, rewired. It's as simple as this: our brains are changing. A woman's thoughts, her ability to focus, and the amount of fuel going to the intuitive centers in the temporal lobes of her brain all are plugged into, and affected by, the circuits being rewired." ~Dr. Christian Northrup

I had never really experienced anxiety, other than not feeling confident, which I think is very different. I didn't know that anxiety could come with hot flashes. This was so different. This anxiety was an anxiety where I wanted to crawl out of my skin. I couldn't control it and I didn't know why or when it would come and then it would be gone. I remember students who tried to describe their anxiety. I couldn't truly understand until I felt it myself. *Why was God doing this now? Was this part of some plan to help my soul grow? Why couldn't I relax and enjoy life? Why do I feel compelled all the time to keep learning?*

"Instantly I comprehend the truth of these thoughts. Reality is the present. Dwelling in the past or future causes pain and illness. Patience can stop time. God's love is everything." *Brian Weiss speaks to my soul.*

Why does someone else's writing in a book seem so much more powerful than me sharing my story? Why do I feel Brian Weiss's words are more important than my words?

A man speaks to us as we are walking on the beach. "People used to wear pigtails in the 50's. You don't see that much anymore, you know?" We stop and for a brief moment, I sense my father's presence. This often happens when I talk to older gentlemen. I tell him that I am glad I could remind him of those times. I love wearing my pigtail braids!

I go for a run- my mind won't stop. I need to get back and write everything down. It's like a dam has opened and I want to catch every single drop of water all at once. What if I forget some of the thoughts I have when I am running; all that water slipping through my hands. The words gone before I can put them on paper; only traveling through my mind but I couldn't catch them quick enough. I must try to slow down and enjoy the process, like real life action research. There are no deadlines as time marches on. "The dime story is always within me," a voice assures me.

I'm in no hurry when I run. I'm not tracking myself on a device and have no idea how far or how long I run. I run, turn around and come back. A few people say good morning and a few of the other runners nod their head in my direction. I stop and do some yoga on the beach. I am breathing in the air from the ocean as the waves roll in. How exhilarating! I am trying to be confident. I have been doing yoga since I started my new job a year ago and I know how to do some poses. I falter on one pose, wondering if anyone saw me and possibly judged me about my yoga. I am trying to steady my pose when a woman walks by and says, "Good place to do that." Her words are not lost. I remember them quite clearly.

I hear Anita Moorjani's voice,

"The only way to heal the physical body is from within. It isn't from food, medical techniques. You and you alone can heal yourself."

Can this be true? I wonder how.... I think what she means is that I need to feel God's love inside me. I need to listen to the positive voice, not the doubting voice. The choice is mine.

This is exhausting. When I eat healthy foods and am open to receiving messages, signs consume me more and I find God everywhere I turn. My intuition is turned up on high. I sit on our patio after our walk. My mind is full of thoughts- how will I possibly remember them all? I can't seem to write fast enough. The caretaker of the condo is walking nearby, spraying something between the cracks of the cement. I say, "Good Morning!" He jumps and says, "Oh! I was talking to myself. So much on my mind to remember. I have to get it all into my brain, you know what I mean?" as he points to his head similar to the way the Wizard of Oz scarecrow does when he says he doesn't have a brain. *Yeah, I think, I know exactly what you mean. Seriously? How does this guy say exactly what I was writing about? I don't even know him! Is it a sign from God? I have so much to write about and yet I haven't even started sharing about the dimes. This story is so much more than the dimes. I worry that when I start to talk about the dimes, the story will unfold yet I might not have looked inside myself enough to be healed. I have so much to share! But, who will want to listen?*

Day by day, wave by wave, trying my best to stay in the present moment, as that is where there is Heaven on Earth; or, at least that is what Anita says can be true. *I drink my probiotic. Will it help heal my gut? Can I truly digest all of the information I am receiving this week? Am I healing through the writing and the healthy food I am eating and drinking? A voice inside tells me this is what I need to do. How do I know if this voice is coming from Spirit, like intuition or something? Is this something to do with being an empath or is it my brain? I find that if I don't listen to the voice, I will hear the message more than once. For instance, someone mentions cutting down on their coffee. Ok, that's fine, but then another message comes about coffee. Usually by the second or third time, I know it is not just coincidence. I am meant to hear the message- like a tape replaying over and over again in my head until I listen. The universe speaks to us. What does Anita say about food? She thinks it doesn't matter, but my mind says- use both ways to heal. Heal with food and through emotions. I will continue this journey with both and have faith that I will be healed.*

Most people might not know by looking at me that I struggle with food and my weight. At one point in my life I lost almost 60 pounds. At 5 ft 4inches, I was close to 185 pounds. It's not that I want to be toothpick skinny; I don't want to keep gaining weight. It seemed that no matter what I did, I kept gaining more and more weight. I saw women all around me happy with their bodies, no matter their size. For me, it isn't about dieting to the point that I don't enjoy life or that everything I eat is either good or bad. I wanted to enjoy life and not feel like I was on a diet. Health was my goal so that I could enjoy the next step of my life's journey. I wouldn't be able to do that if I kept getting fatter and fatter. I want to be me in a regular sized body. *Would I ever be able to do this? Was I scared of being fat like my mother? Would being fat lead me to heart disease, like both of my parents?*

I don't think my Mother was scared of dying. She always said she didn't want to be in a nursing home, where others would have to care for her. It made sense towards the end that she didn't want medical help. I believe she knew exactly what she was doing when she wouldn't get help that year. Right before Thanksgiving of 2014, I watched her as she began to take on fluid from her congestive heart failure. When confronted, she refused to talk about it and eventually told me that she, "wasn't going to be in the hospital for the holidays." I had no argument for that. I understood and tried to help her and dad during the next month as much as I could. At this point, it was difficult for her to think straight. We had sold the family business and, ever since then, she didn't know what to do with herself. My Grandfather had started that business in 1933. My parents had owned and operated the business together for many years. That was her life and I think she didn't know what to do with herself without her work. She enjoyed seeing the customers who all had become friends over the years.

I remember being extremely patient with her while I helped her buy Christmas presents- a scarf for every girl in our family. We bought them the day before Thanksgiving, when I drove her and my dad to the city of Montpelier. Dad needed to renew his license (he probably shouldn't have been driving but I did not have the nerve or heart to tell him) and Mom had a JC Penney coupon she wanted to use. These scarves were one of the last personal gifts she would ever give to all of us girls. I remember walking with her in the store that day. She stopped about every 10-15 feet to breathe. She looked at me and stated that she needed to go slower. I gladly slowed down to walk with her, while dad waited in the car. *Patience. Slow down. Be present. All lessons I need to learn again and again.*

In early December of 2014, I called a few of my Mom's close friends to share my concerns about her declining health. I was worried something would happen to her in the night and my Dad would try to get help, but it wouldn't be quick enough. I was scared she might die right in their bed. Thoughts came back from the last time she was rushed to the hospital with congestive heart failure. My husband tried to warn me that maybe I shouldn't be calling everyone, but I listened to my intuition, the voice inside- *was this God's way of speaking to me? Does God speak to empaths somehow?* Those friends were so grateful for my phone calls. These friends reached out to her in her last few days. Whether it was a phone call or bringing Mom some of her favorite soup on her birthday; it meant a lot to Mom and to them.

We had a great day celebrating Christmas that year with Mom and Dad. We set aside the Saturday after Christmas to have an afternoon with only desserts, no big meal. My father loved desserts! I stopped by one evening prior to our visit. Dad asked me when those presents we got were going to be wrapped. Mom had said she would do it and I didn't realize that it was too much for her at the time. This would be the last time I would see them before our Christmas celebration. Well, I guess I could do it right now, I suggested. I was worried about stepping on Mom's toes, not wanting her to lose some of her independence in life. Although it was late and I wanted to get home, I got out all of the supplies and started to wrap the presents.

While wrapping, I listened to my parent's banter about dinner. At that point, Mom wasn't really able to prepare dinner; something she had always done. Dad began to get his own dinner, eating something that Mom did not approve of. She often told him what to eat and what not to eat. Mom prepared herself an apple and cheese. She brought her plate into the dining room, where I was beginning to wrap the presents. She sat down, breathing like she had climbed Mount Everest. She wasn't even able to talk. This is how congestive heart failure works. The heart valve doesn't work properly, allowing for the extra fluid to be dumped into the lungs. The person feels like they can't breathe, fooling them into thinking that they will get better if they could breathe.

"But I trust in you, O Lord; I say, 'You are my God.' My times are in your hands." Psalm 31:14-15

I wonder how much longer she has left? Why won't she go get help? My thoughts wander as I wrap the presents she is to give to everyone in a few days. I try to be present but I'm always thinking about things in my head. Why am I like this? Always thinking of the next thing I have to do. Difficulty being in the moment. I guess when I was younger it was always easier to be in my head than my body. This was a skill that I was super good at. It helped me be able to ignore my feelings.

When we celebrated Christmas that year, my sons would have their picture taken with both sets of their Grandparents, not realizing later how much those pictures would mean to all of us. My boys were lucky to have two sets of Grandparents for their entire childhood. I wish all kids were able to feel the love from a Grandparent. *A Grandparent's love feels like love from God, a voice whispers. Anything given by a Grandparent is also filled with love. The most significant dime was given to my son, from his Grandfather. Without that dime, I never would have written this book.*

"Our thoughts are silent words that only we and the Lord hear, but those words affect our inner man, our health, our joy, and our attitude." ~ Joyce Meyer

Chapter 7 "Come What May"

"You cannot control what happens to you in life, but you can always control what you will feel and do about what happens to you," ~ Viktor E. Frankl

"It is now well documented that the electromagnetic field of the heart is 5,000 times more powerful than the electromagnetic field of the brain. And that is why, no matter what we think, what we actually feel is what matters most. Every time. No exceptions. You might be able to fool your brain, but you can't fool your heart." ~Dr. Christian Northrup, from www.heartmath.org

I never felt like my Mother gave me her approval for any of my accomplishments. When I would talk about my son hitting a double in a little league all star game, she would change the subject. I would talk about my new job; she would talk about a customer from their business. I never quite understood this part of her. As I reflected on my relationship with my mother, I watched as she slowly began to slip away from us.

What would my life be like without her? I had spent most of my life angry with her. Would all my pain and feelings disappear when she was gone? Would I ever be free to be happy with myself as I was? Did I need my mother's approval to make me whole? I know how important it was

to face my feelings because I didn't want to end up with heart disease like my parents. And, if my feelings were what was going to determine this, I needed to work not just on being healthy, but dealing with my own internal pain. I was fighting an uphill battle. I had dreams of playing with my grandkids. I didn't want my kids to have to take care of me when I was ailing, like I had with my parents. I needed to get healthy by eating better, exercising and dealing with my feelings. It had to start now or else it would be too late.

I bought a ring the fall of 2014, when I saw my parents' health worsening. It said "Come What May" on it and was meaningful to me because I thought my parents might not make it through the winter. *Should I listen to my intuition? What if I was wrong? Was my intuition part of being an empath? Could I have a sense of what the future might hold? Wasn't everything in God's plan?* I knew that whatever happened, I was going to need to pray to be able to get through it. I was going to have to take it as it came, whatever that may be. As the common sayings go, "what will be will be" or "it is what it is". Whatever "it" was, I was going to need God's help.

On Dec. 30th, 2014 my father panicked. Mom wasn't "acting right". He told my sister and uncle that somebody had to come over right away; he didn't know what to do.

This same situation had happened previously in the summer as well. He phoned people to come over to help. When I arrived at their camp that day, Mom was belligerent and not cooperating with the rescue squad *or anyone*. She had diabetes and her blood sugar was dangerously low. After her heart surgery, she had been diagnosed with Type 2 Diabetes. She tried to manage her insulin levels with medicine, but not usually with food. I tried to help her learn how to eat healthier, but she would only make small changes, not big changes.

Last summer at camp, after trying to get her to cooperate, I told her that it was morning and it was time for her orange juice. She always had one small glass of orange juice every morning with her coffee. We even put it in a small cup. She was in bed and I got into bed with her. I remember the look in her eyes as I held her tight with my arm around her neck, hugging her and began pouring the orange juice into her mouth, which she barely opened. On some level, she knew to trust me; but, at the time, she was out of her mind. I remember the look in her eyes. *Was she going to trust me? She wouldn't listen to anyone. She wouldn't cooperate with anyone else.* She drank the little bit of orange juice and it helped. She was then able to walk to the car to go to the hospital. *I don't think Mom remembers what happened, but I knew this was one of the only times in my life where I was able to help my mother. Most of the time she seemed to refuse my help and love.*

When my uncle called me that December 30th, I was already on my way to my parents' house. I was planning on stopping by for lunch on my way through town to an acupuncture appointment. When I arrived, Mom was in the bathroom and Dad quietly reported that she had been there most of the morning. Dad greeted me with tears in his eyes and I wasn't exactly sure what I was going to do. I had phoned the doctor's office, to report her condition. The receptionist was a member of our extended family and I knew she couldn't talk to me about Mom, but I could talk to her. I explained to her that Mom had been taking on fluid since Thanksgiving and she wasn't acting right. I told her I would be in touch after I visited. She would wait to hear from me and was ready to help.

I had brought my lunch and began preparing my parents a lunch also. Mom demanded that her soup be in a coffee cup, not a bowl. *What does it matter? I thought to myself. Whatever she wants I thought, but nothing seemed to make her happy.* She wasn't sure what Dad should eat, seeming sort of confused. In and out of the bathroom she went. She tried to eat, but then ended up back in the living room. Dad and I finished eating and now they were both sitting in their recliners in the corners of the living room. *That's when the scene unfolded. A conversation that had been put on hold until after the holidays. Now was the time for us to face Mom's reality.*

Mom said to me, "I don't know why you had to rush right down here". I stopped dead in my tracks, at the edge of the living room and proceeded to throw words right back at her, "I don't have any idea what you are talking about. I am on my way to an acupuncture appointment. I stopped in for lunch to see you both."

That is when I stopped, thought and glared back at my mother. I was standing with one foot still in the living room and one foot in the room that would be my escape route out of the house. The board that separated the two rooms was a nice piece of cherry wood from my Great Grandfather's farm. *Was he there helping me help my father and mother? I wonder as I write.* I looked back across the living room at both of my parents sitting in their recliners on the other side of the room. *Should I stay or should I go? Which foot should I follow? It would be so much easier to walk away. I knew it wasn't ok to take the easy route. My father needed my help and my mother didn't seem to want my help.*

My Mother hadn't told anyone that she was ill. She didn't want to go to the hospital; she had already told me that. But, the holidays were over and it was time she got some help. Her eyes met mine. *Should I continue to my appointment or face her right now and demand she go to the hospital? What should I say to her? I'm the child. She is the parent. I shouldn't speak back to my parents, right? Growing up that hadn't worked for me. Was I going to be able to face the mother who I felt did not understand me?*

I stood still and thought to myself, *"I guess it is now or never so here goes nothing! Time to face this"*- something I rarely felt the courage to do *with my mother.* The words I spoke next came from the positive voice inside me- the one that isn't afraid to speak the truth- no matter what it is. I began to explain to her that we all cared about her. She wasn't used to hearing this. *"You want to know what is happening? That man (my Dad cried as I pointed towards him) loves you very much. We all want you to go get the medical help you need. In fact, a lot of people around here love you very much."* The voice inside me at that moment was the positive voice, my intuition guiding me, telling me what I needed to do at that particular moment. Switch the argument and fighting to love and caring. That's the answer.

These words were rarely spoken when I was growing up. My whole life I had been searching for my mother's love. I had held onto my anger and even though I had tried over the years, I hadn't showed my mother much love. *If I showed my mother that I loved her, would she, in return, give me the love I so longed for?* She agreed that it would probably be ok to call the doctor's office.

I sat on the couch and called the doctor's office. *"Hi. This is Monica. I'm sitting here with Mom and she isn't feeling very well. We thought maybe she should see the doctor today."* The secretary knew the situation so I didn't need to explain further. With that, she gave me two options. I could come now (which meant I would miss my acupuncture appointment) or at 3:30, which meant I could still go to my appointment and then come back later to take her to the doctor. At the time, I felt like I made a selfish choice, but now I see that it was meant to be. I had listened to my intuition and made the choice that would, in the end, be the best choice. That afternoon would be the last time that my Dad would be able to talk with my Mother. That afternoon they talked about a lot of things. Later, I would learn my mother gave me her "approval" that afternoon.

When I arrived back from my appointment, Mom was sitting in the chair in the dining room, the spot where she always put on her shoes. Dad, with tears in his eyes watched as Mom tried to put on her socks and shoes, unable to bend over. I helped her. One sock. One shoe. Other sock. Other shoe. *Role reversal again. I felt like I was the parent caring for the child.* She had trouble standing up; Dad and I helped her. Out of breath from the exertion of standing up, my parents kiss and say I love you to each other. This scene was rare in my family. Growing up, I never really saw my parents be affectionate with each other. I helped Mom put on her coat, then went to move the van so that it would be easier to get her into the car. They had a precious minute alone. It was difficult getting Mom into the car. I helped her so that she could sit on the seat, but it left her legs sticking straight out of the van. Her legs were so swollen with fluid, her knees were barely able to bend. I backed up the seat and one by one, lifted her legs into the car by grabbing the top of her pants. I was so focused on getting Mom into the car, I have no idea what it must have felt like for Dad to be left alone in the house; watching me load her into the car and worrying about his wife of almost 60 years.

We made it to the doctor's office; Mom greets our relative and the doctor as if this is a normal appointment. The doctor seems shy and asks Mom what is going on. Mom doesn't give a whole lot of details. *I think about the past month. We had to buy her bigger pants because of the fluid. She doesn't even eat much but she keeps getting bigger. She can barely walk she is so out of breath. Should I tell the doctor about her legs not bending when I tried to help her in the car? I don't want to embarrass her, but I think her condition is pretty serious.*

The doctor does the usual blood pressure check and makes small talk about the weather. At one point in the conversation, Mom had almost convinced the doctor that it would probably be ok if she went home. I remember thinking, *"Oh, My God, what is going on here? Am I crazy? What about getting her heart checked out or possibly staying overnight to be monitored?"* I tried to listen to my intuition and allow the doctor to help us, but I also needed to make sure he knew how bad she really was. She wasn't acting like she had been at home with Dad. *How would I make sure she got the proper medical help she needed?*

Finally, they both agree that maybe she could spend one night and see what happened. *Phew, I think.* We wheeled her over to the emergency room to be admitted to the hospital. The look on the nurse's face when she took a quick peek at Mom's legs was all I needed to see to know that Mom was right where she needed to be. Her skin was so tight it looked like her skin was about to pop open. Mom would be given medicine to begin to try to get rid of the fluid.

Mom and I talked about everything and nothing all afternoon while we waited for a hospital room. She asked me about school and our plans for New Year's Eve. There were some distractions, including one of my students in the ER with his brother, who had broken his arm skiing. Mom would get to meet him and she loved that. I remember her asking him if I was a good teacher. What was he supposed to say with me standing right there? We had what I call "surface conversations". Talking about things that don't matter much. No deep conversations like, *"What if I might die? Or What about Dad?"* We talked more about the weather and people who worked at the hospital. That's the way my Mom was with me.

After settling Mom into her room and stopping by to visit my Dad, I went home. I wish I had stayed that night with Dad, but it wasn't meant to be. The phone rang at 4:00 AM at his house. He was disoriented and confused- trying to hear without his hearing aids. He couldn't understand why someone was asking him if he would need the police to give him a ride to the hospital. From there, the phone calls would bring everyone to the hospital to find that Mom had "coded" and they had done life saving techniques until the family arrived. She was breathing but nothing was happening "neurologically" speaking. The decision was made and we were guided to let her go; a decision that haunted my father. He thought we had made the wrong decision to let her go. He was scared of death and had fought his own heart disease for most of his life. Mom and Dad had a secret code when he would have his heart surgeries. The secret message would be three squeezes or 3 movements of the arm or hand. Three squeezes meant that they were still alive and responding. To them it meant, "don't give up on me." Because Mom's arm had signaled (she had slammed her arm down), he thought it was a message from her to not let her die. In the moment, I felt that Mom didn't want all of this attention around her and she didn't want to live like this. It was like she threw her fist in anger. To Dad, it was a totally different sign. I wouldn't discover this until later; Dad never shared this at the hospital. His experience was different than mine based on our differing views.

We all congregated in the ICU hallway while the hospital staff removed the machines that were keeping Mom alive. *What does one say during a time like this? To me, the memory is a blur. So much to think about.* The family gathers around her bed. With all of the machines gone, Mom was barely breathing. We all talked to Mom and told her it was ok. Within minutes, her heart stopped beating and she took her last breath.

I can see her taking her last breath and then my eyes immediately focus on my Father. Sitting in his wheelchair, crying uncontrollably. I had never seen my father like this. *What should I do? How do I take care of him?* My adrenaline kicks in and I know that this will be very difficult for my father. Decisions will need to be made and my father will need help. *My life was about to change and I was about to discover some hidden coins, which would begin to uncover my true beliefs about life and death; helping me to heal from the inside out.*

My strength would be tested many times and, in due time, my father would help me to have faith in believing that people can really connect with people who have died. There really is a spirit communication available to those who want to use it. Would my mother contact me now? Would she be different as a spirit? Would I be able to forgive her? Did she try her best with what she was given? Were my expectations too much for her?

"Holding onto anger is like drinking poison and hoping the other person will die." ~Buddha

Anger and resentment eat away at my insides every day, if I let it. Now she is gone, what will happen to my anger? How will I be able to avoid heart disease? That is one of the first questions doctors ask you, "Any heart disease in the family?" Yeah- both my parents....Turning 50, I was wondering how to live differently to avoid the emotional pain that affects my physical body, possibly following in my mother and father's footsteps of heart disease.

"I didn't get to grow up and pull away from her and bitch about her with my friends and confront her about the things I'd wished she'd done differently and then get older and understand that she had done the best she could and realize that what she had done was pretty damn good and take her fully back into my arms again. Her death had obliterated that. It had obliterated me. It had cut me short at the very height of my youthful arrogance. It had forced me

Me hiking in North Carolina.

to instantly grow up and forgive her every motherly fault at the same time that it kept me forever a child, my life both ended and begun in that premature place where we'd left off. She was my mother, but I was motherless. I was trapped by her, but utterly alone. She would always be the empty bowl that no one could fill. I'd have to fill it myself again and again and again." ~Cheryl Strayed

Chapter 8 Time with My Dad

"Regardless of any overt risks we may have for heart disease (such as poor diet or lack of exercise), the seeds for potentially developing heart disease later on are sown the minute we learn to start shutting down our hearts to avoid feeling disappointment and loss. Whether or not heart disease eventually results has a lot to do with how well we learn how to feel and express our emotions fully and name the needs they signify." ~Dr. Christian Northrup

Faith in God will heal me. I think as I envision a healthy heart within me.

Had my father's heart been broken since that first heart attack when I was 13? What broke it? Would he be able to heal it this late in life? Would losing his wife break his heart even more or could he be able to live differently now to change his path? Even though diet and exercise are important, how was I going to learn to be able to express my feelings? When I was studying for my master's degree, information about the newest brain research fascinated me. Would I be able to change my brain in time to avoid heart disease? There were so many connections that were hard wired into my brain when I was young, how was I going to reprogram them? How long would it take to make them a habit? Where do I even start?

"Every thought of yours is a real thing- a force." ~ Prentice Mulford (1834-1891)

When I was young, I would get home from school and my go-to snack was Sprite and Cheez Doodles or pretzels. My Mom kept a large supply of soda on hand all of the time. On top of our fridge a variety of different salty snacks would be piled high. Fritos, pretzels, Cheez Doodles, Doritoes, Cheetos and more. We never had any fruit out on the counter, ever. Once in awhile there would be an apple or an orange in the fridge, but we were never encouraged to eat them so they would get soft and nasty. There wasn't as much of a focus on eating healthy when I was growing up; or, at least, not in my family. My brain was hard wired into thinking this is what a person ate when transitioning from school to home. As an adult, I attempted to change my habits to make more healthy choices. I was undoing years of conditioning around food. *My writing seems to flow better when I eat healthy but, so do my emotions. Why is this a problem? Well, because I don't know how to feel my emotions and I don't know what to do with them. Eating carbs or junk food helps me to not feel anything, kind of numbing me and making me feel safer. It actually closes up my throat so that I am not able to breath deeply. When that happens, I lose touch with my center. I lose touch with my inner voice that seems to come from someplace else.*

"Your life's journey has been perfectly designed for you soul's growth. Embrace every lesson and every moment."~ Dr. Judith Orloff

Recently I saw a sign at a farmer's market. It read, "Eat like your life depended on it." I thought, that makes a lot of sense. *Then I thought, "Think like your life depended on it." How do I change every negative thought into a positive thought? Start small, one thought at a time. I am writing a book and it is going to be a good book. There, my anxiety begins to subside. Not gone, but it's a start.*

After my Mother died, I decided to take a leave of absence from teaching to care for my father. This was a very difficult decision as I loved my new job as a middle school Math teacher. The Curriculum Director told me, "I have never met anyone who regretted taking time to be with their parents." Over the next few months, my life revolved around Dad. This meant I didn't take the time to grieve for my Mom. I was too busy caring for my Dad around the clock since he had taken a bad fall the night my mother died.

Trying to console my father was difficult for me. I was consumed with taking care of my father, funeral arrangements, and paper work involved with my Mother's death. He had lost his wife, his true love of almost 60 years. *How could I possibly help someone through this? Especially my father.* I thank God everyday for Dad's best friend, Eldon, arriving to stay with us. He would help my father, as he had lost his wife a few years before. The support was invaluable. I didn't know much about grief and Eldon explained the different stages. I printed information about the stages of grief for my dad to read, but ultimately it was this friendship that would help him get through that first week without Mom. Our families were so connected over the years. It was like I had another Father that week.

I remember serving these two friends dinner. Dad wanted to pay for the flight to Vermont. Eldon had flown up from Florida in the middle of winter to be with Dad during this time. During dinner, he looked across the table at my father and said, "I really don't want you to pay for my flight. You have to understand that our friendship is priceless to me. You can't put a price on it. If you want to do something with money, give a donation to the Lamoille Area Cancer Network, in honor of my wife." With tears in his eyes, my father agrees. We were eating lasagna, both men were missing their wives and thankful for their friendship. I can feel the energy of tremendous love these two men had for each other and their families. *This is what is happening as I unfold my story. When*

I write and think back to some of those moments in time, I sense a strong energy. At the time, I thought it was the love between these two men. Now, I understand that it was more than that. It was both of their wives, in the room with us. I can feel it as I write.

We had many laughs and many tears that week, reminiscing. We cried because my Mom wouldn't get the medical help she so desperately needed. We laughed when Eldon told me how fast he ran down the grass bank at camp after I had knocked myself out by skiing head first into the dock. He was so scared. For me, all I remembered was I was skiing on one ski for the first time and I wanted to try to spray my brother sitting in the boat near the dock. The next thing I knew, I was lying down in camp with something on my head, listening to his daughter whine that she didn't want to go home. I remember all of my early life memories of playing Barbies, swimming and such. I did all that with her; she was my best friend. Along with reminiscing the fun times together, Eldon taught me how to put toilet paper on correctly, that OJ is served with ice and when you have a chocolate dessert, you serve white milk or, if you have a white dessert, you serve chocolate milk. It was a time to grieve, laugh, heal and begin to process a new way of life. For my father, life would be different without his wife by his side. I would move back in to the home where I grew up to care for my father for as long as he needed me.

I would begin sharing some of my insights about life, afterlife, signs and such with my father. He slowly started to feel it. A tipped lampshade? He thought it was my Mom doing that. I was told to straighten it out immediately.He would say that she didn't like it tipped. He thought she was still angry all the time, like she had been the past few years. When she was sick over the last few years, it was difficult for her to think clearly. Oftentimes, she would be difficult to deal with. It wasn't her fault. Her mind wasn't able to work like she wanted it to. One time she said, "It's like my thinker doesn't work anymore." *I can imagine how difficult it must be growing old. We begin to lose pieces of ourselves.*

I tried to explain to him that Heaven was different. All human problems were gone. I'm not sure he ever quite understood.

"Pain, like fever, is a symptom. It is also a vital component of the human experience." ~Margaret A. Caudill M.D.

When I was trying to heal my root chakra (the area at the base of the spine that relates to your sense of security and safety) after my back surgery in 1996, the traditional medical doctors were unable to help me. They removed a herniated disc on my right side at the L5/SI joint. It was perhaps the worst, but eventually the best time in my life. I didn't heal as expected and went in to a deep depression. My kids were one and three at the time and I was unable to care for them. This literally broke my heart as I loved being a Mom. I was barely able to function and losing my job became a strong possibility. I looked to the doctors for help and they wanted me to take some pills to "relax me". I remember the pill well. It was called amitriptyline. I took one pill and proceeded to be "out of my mind". I remember screaming- yes screaming at my older son. I remember my promise to myself that when I became a mom I was going to mother my children differently than the way I was mothered. I can't remember what I screamed at him for but no three year old should have to endure that type of treatment. I realized what I was doing as I had an out of body experience. I watched from above as I screamed at my son. *Would I let others ever treat my son like this? Absolutely not. So, why was it ok for me to do this? It wasn't.* After I screamed at him I walked back to the kitchen, took the bottle out of the cupboard and dumped the entire bottle of pills down the toilet. Never was I going to let this happen again. I then walked back to my son, scooped him up in my arms and rocked him in a chair. I prayed for God to help me find a different way to heal my pain. Luckily, soon after this I was introduced to alternative healing techniques; such as massage therapy, Reiki, and chiropractic care. *The only problem was once I learned about these ways to heal, I only did them when pain was interfering in my life. I did not practice them on a daily basis.*

The answer to my prayer came soon after that time. There happened to be an evening meeting in town on how to manage pain. I have no idea how I found out about it, but I went and began to learn how to deal with pain in a very different way. I learned about our body's natural relaxation response. When we breathe from our belly, our body automatically relaxes. After that one meeting, I began trying alternative methods of healing. This included Reiki, massage, acupuncture, network chiropractic and learning to breathe for meditation. The worst part of my life had turned out to be the best thing in the end. I learned how to care for myself in a very different way.

While trying to heal recently, I was given the drug amitriptyline again by another doctor. The urologist told me that it would help relieve my bladder pain. I was told by the doctor to "Just keep taking more and more until I don't feel the pain anymore". At this point, I hadn't slept well in months and was desperate to sleep. I followed the doctor's orders. It didn't work. *Was I surprised? Well, not really.* I decided to stop taking them. *Did I need to revisit what I had learned from my back surgery years ago? Was this God's message to me that I needed to keep searching for different answers to help myself heal? Was I going to finally have to get honest with myself and admit that I didn't love myself? How would I do this? I had read all of the books and inspirational quotes that explained that positive self talk was important to my healing. I had all of the tools, how would I be able to begin to use them wholeheartedly in my life? How would I change my daily life to include these?*

"Let go of the difficulties from your past, cultural codes, and social beliefs. You are the only one who can create the life you deserve." ~from The Secret by Rhonda Byrne

I sneeze all the time. If anyone has ever heard me sneeze, they know that I don't sneeze one at a time. I do little ach-oos over and over again; sometimes 5 or 6 times. I'm not sick when I sneeze. I'm not even stuffy or having an allergy attack. When teaching, I used to joke with my students, saying, "I think I am allergic to you." Actually, I began to think that I was allergic to certain foods. That is, until I read Mallika

Chopra's book, Living with Intent My Somewhat Messy Journey to Purpose, Peace and Joy. She was Deepok Chopra's daughter! *How could her life be messy? Didn't having a father like hers make it a given that she too would automatically be perfect? I mean, Deepok must have taught her so much. Imagine having a father like that! I think that might have made my life so much easier.* Then, I read her book and found out that she, like me, was finding her way in the game of life. But, one thing stuck out for me in her book. She was about to meet Eckart Tolle and had been sneezing for hours before the meeting.

"It hits me that while I sat with Eckhart, I didn't sneeze at all. I was feeling truly peaceful and in the present moment." ~Mallika Chopra

Wait, could her thoughts have been making her sneeze? For me, was it my thoughts or the actual food I was eating? Again, I think of Anita Moorjani talking about emotions being stronger than the food we eat. I begin tracking my thoughts when I sneeze. Oh my....yes, it's true. Every time I sneeze, my thoughts were something like, "I shouldn't be eating this cookie. It's going to make me fat." Or "You need to make a better choice. Say no to the social pressure of having cake. Why aren't you stronger?" Could this really be? Was I seriously allergic to my thoughts and not what-ever was in the cookie or cake? Sometimes, it wouldn't be about food, but a general negative thought. I begin the slow journey of changing my thoughts into positive thoughts and I sneeze less and less. Instead of thinking I shouldn't be eating some things, I bless the food and am grateful for all food I am given. Changing the hard wires in my brain became a full time job. I think of my father as he wants to work on his physical body like a car engine. I had to feed my engine the fuel it needed to run the way it was meant to run. For me this meant eating God's food from earth, not man made processed food.

"Any time you look at yourself with critical eyes, switch your focus immediately to the *presence* within, and its perfection will reveal itself to You. As you do this, all imperfections that have man-ifested in your life will dissolve, because imperfections cannot exist

in the light of this presence. **Whether you want to regain perfect eyesight, dissolve disease and restore well-being, turn poverty into abundance, reverse again and degeneration, or eradicate any negativity, focus on and love the presence within you and perfection will manifest."** ~Rhonda Byrne

Well, I didn't need "perfection"; any improvement would be great! *Would I be able to make these new wires a permanent part of my brain? Would changing my inner dialogue from negative self talk to positive self talk heal my physical pain? It's been two years since I read Mallika's book. "Think like your life depends on it." The saying repeats over and over in my mind. I knew I had to believe that God was inside me, healing me with my thoughts.*

"Recognizing emotion means developing awareness about how our thinking, feeling (including our physiology), and behavior are connected... I have seen no evidence in my research that real transformation happens until we address all three as equally important parts of a whole." ~ *Brene Brown*

My father heard me speak of alternative ways to heal over the years. He wanted to try them, but never had the chance or never dared to. While staying with him, I asked if he wanted to try Reiki or acupuncture. He did! *Would I be able to share alternative healing techniques with my father? He wanted to try other things to heal. He was nervous and had so many questions.*

I called up a friend and asked if she would be willing to come to my father's house to give him a Reiki session. My Dad was nervous and asked a zillion questions. Our conversation went something like this:

"Would it be like a massage?" *No, she puts her hands on you but only touches you. No pushing into your muscles.*

"Will it hurt?" *No, you might feel hot or cold.*

"What does hot or cold mean?" *There is no science to Reiki. It is energy based healing and I can't really explain it to you. You have to feel it and then see how much better you feel after. It works better if you relax and believe that it will help you.*

"How will I know if it worked?" *You'll enjoy the experience and hope that it helps your pain.*

And the questions went on and on like a three year old asking Why? He wondered how his human engine would heal with this type of servicing.

My Dad's first Reiki session goes very well. He sleeps better that night and can't believe how relaxed he felt. He describes the sensation in his legs. "It was like she took all the energy out of my body and it shot down my legs and disappeared right out my feet. How does that work?" It wasn't like a car engine where one knew that when someone changed the oil, the engine would run better. This was an energy that you couldn't see or explain. *You had to believe.* I smile and know that some of the energy and emotions stored in his body for years was released. His engine had been partially cleaned out. After that first session, he kept asking when, "hot hands" was coming back. He couldn't remember her name but knew her hands were hot.

When Dad receives his second Reiki treatment, I remember back to a guided visual meditation I had during a training for Reiki. It was about a year after my back surgery. I remember the vision clearly. I was told to envision my favorite place and imagine myself there. I was in such a relaxed state that my inner mind took over. *Was this the voice inside my head that came from somewhere else? Had I tapped into it during the meditation?* I was swimming like a loon. I dove deep down in the water and shot across the lake. When I popped up out of the water, my Grandmother Palmer (my father's mother) was there, ready to embrace me in a God Love hug. She wasn't like I remembered her. She was much younger. I remember that hug as my father receives his Reiki. *I wonder where my father's mind goes when he gets Reiki? Does he fall asleep? Does he have any visions? I never told anyone about my vision of swimming deep in the water. Would he dare to say anything if something happened in his mind during his treatment?*

Dad had a few more sessions with her and then his nerves got the best of him after a treatment. At one point in the session, he said that his heart felt funny. He was worried that whatever she was doing was going to be bad for his heart. His heart doctor had reassured him that Reiki was good for him and that it wouldn't "hurt" him. Dad wasn't convinced. He decided to stop having Reiki but started asking about acupuncture.

I set up an appointment with my acupuncturist to come to the house for a home treatment. This would be the same person who had supported me when I lost my Mom. Dad had questions. I was only able to explain some of the answers to him. Sarah decided to do a small, short treatment for his first time. Dad reported that it was hogwash and he didn't feel a thing. "I'm not spending money on that. It didn't do anything!" This would be the end of his trying alternative therapies. He would go back to the Western medical world to try to help him deal with his ailments. *If only he had been able to experience this years ago. Would he be happier? Would he have been able to live longer? I wanted to help him, but it was ultimately his choice whether or not to try alternative healing. I couldn't make him do it.*

While living with my father, I noticed how different our diets were. For awhile, my Dad received the Meals on Wheels program in town. They would deliver a meal every weekday. While I was making vegetable soup and eating fruit, Dad was giving all of the vegetables in his meal to me. He wouldn't eat butter, but would eat margarine. I realized as an adult, I had changed my eating habits so much compared to what I had eaten when I was young.

While living with my father that winter, I had talked about the possibility of getting a cat. Years ago, when my Mom was sick the first time, my younger son had said to me, "Mom. I don't want to be mean or anything and I don't hope that Grandma passes away. But, if she does, can we get Grandpa a kitty?" See, my Father loved visiting our home because we always had cats at our house. I talked about adopting a cat and my father would brush me off. He bragged about the picture of him when he was a kid. He was holding a cat in one hand and a bird in the other hand. I knew he would love having a cat. This cat would become the angel Dad needed in his life.

Dad with a cat on his left shoulder and a bird on his right hand.

Here is Dad's "pet" bird on his head!

I found an older cat and the rescue adoption process began; with the understanding that if it didn't work out, the cat would move to my house. When I think of the word rescue, I originally thought that we were rescuing the cat. *But I think the cat rescued Dad.* Once that cat moved into Dad's house, that cat never belonged to me. Once the cat was comfortable (which took so long!), she was our entertainment and Dad's angel. Dad was more patient waiting for the cat to settle in than I was. She had stayed in the bathroom for days, only daring to go between the bathroom and the cat litter box. You could tell she had had a traumatic experience and was very scared.

This is the cat Dad and I adopted, Missy.

It was so exciting that first night she made a trip to the living room. Dad and I were sitting in the recliners in the corners of the living room watching TV. Missy, the cat, does a loop around the middle of the house. We almost missed her as she scooted around the corner near the TV. Then she would walk by his chair, eventually working her way to his lap; a perfect friend. Dad considered her a sign from Mom and would share this with a few people. That cat cheered Dad up so much. He was so proud to tell people about "his" cat. He especially liked to watch her eye his "pet" squirrels outside of the window. Birdseed in his bird feeder was actually meant for the squirrels too.

Dad talking to the
Missy.

While looking outside towards the bird feeders that year, our family sees a red cardinal. My mother has red cardinals all over her house. *We wonder, was this her watching over her house?*

I think my father talks to the cat about my mother. I'm not sure, but it feels like he thinks he is connecting with Mom. I wonder if he thinks there is a way to connect with people who have passed on? Is this part of being an empath? Was my father also an empath? Or an animal whisperer? He always joked with my sons that when hunting, my sons should "talk" to the deer.

When Dad was young, he signed up for the Air Force instead of going into the army. He wanted to serve his country. He went to basic training in Texas. Soon after he left, my mother was very sick with rheumatic fever. He was worried about her and the doctors weren't sure if she was going to make it. He came down with his own illness during basic training. He went to the infirmary and they tried to treat the illness. They did not have any luck and one of the doctors decided he needed to go home to be looked at by another doctor. The doctor gave Dad an honorable discharge and my father came home to my mother in the hospital. She did survive but it was touch and go for awhile. I talk with my father about how different our life might have been had he stayed instead of being discharged. He says, "I had never thought about it before." *I wonder to myself, Seriously? Other people don't think about these things? Why am I the one always thinking of how our life journeys are sometimes determined by one single decision or event? What events brought my mother and father together? What happened after he was discharged? This doctor will never know how much this one decision would affect so many lives.*

"No matter what he does, every person on earth plays a central role in the history of the world. And normally he doesn't know it." ~Paul Coelho

My Dad shared lots of stories during our time together. Even though he missed my Mom, he always kept his sense of humor. He sometimes would get short with me, stating that "this wasn't supposed to be a fun time." This was a sad time for him as he missed my Mom dearly. For my family, though, we heard stories that we never got to hear.

When I needed to prick his finger to take a little blood, guess what finger he offered? Or how about the time I had an appointment and my older sister, Debbie, kept asking if he was ready for breakfast. He kept saying no and then the minute I walked through the door, he said, "good thing you are home. She wouldn't feed me!"

Once, while eating dinner, I casually asked him, "Where did that clock come from?"

His response was not what I expected. "That damn thing near killed you!" he replied. "What?" I ask, totally confused.

He repeats, "That thing damn near killed you- you don't remember that? I guess you wouldn't. You were quite little, I guess," he says with a laugh.

I can imagine it in my head as he proceeds to tell me that I was learning how to walk. I was pulling myself up using a bureau. We were at the camp on Lake Elmore. He watched in slow motion as the bureau, with the clock on top, came tumbling down on top of me. He thought it was going to kill me and then proceeded to tell me that the clock had come with the camp, the camp my Great Grandmother had purchased in the 1940's. I now have the clock in my house and my son owns the bureau, a gift from his Grandfather. Stories we had never heard before helped us through our grief.

A touching story about Mom's last birthday was one of the most memorable stories he shared. This would be 8 days before my mother died. When they were headed to bed one night, Mom said to Dad, "You know. I really liked the flowers you got me today but what I really want is a hug." It meant a lot to Dad because my Mom never usually asked for things like that. My Mom didn't really express any emotions around me. My father knew that I was posting some of these stories on Facebook. One day he says to me, "Post that story. It's a good one."

"Each of us takes in at the cellular level how our mother feels about being female, what she believes about her body, how she takes care of her health, and what she believes is possible in life. Her beliefs and behaviors set the tone for how well we learn to care for ourselves as adults. We then pass this information either consciously or unconsciously on to the next generation." ~Dr. Christian Northrup

I wonder if my mother had asked for more physical affection, would she still have died of heart disease? Wouldn't it also have helped my Dad's heart, too? What made her this way? Was it when she almost died from rheumatic fever? Was she so affected by her own father's death that her heart never recovered? Was she always scared that my father would die, like her own father had with his heart attack?

One of the stories Dad told during our time together was about the last afternoon Mom and he had together. They were able to talk about what would happen if she passed. Looking back at the decision I made that afternoon, I can see now that it was meant to be. If I had taken her earlier to the doctors, they wouldn't have had that precious time together. During that afternoon, after I had spoken to my Mom that we all loved her and wanted her to get help, she said to my dad, *"Don't worry. Monica will take care of everything."* Of course, I would not learn this until after my Mother had transitioned to spirit. *I had finally received my mother's approval and now she was gone; only here in spirit.*

Often times, my Dad and I were able to telepathically send messages to each other. I know- visions of Star Wars, the Jetsons or some futuristic alien entered your thoughts. We would be sitting watching TV and I would say something about a doctor's appointment tomorrow. He would respond, "How did you do that? I was going to ask you about that!" He would do the same thing in return. *How does this work I wonder? Is this part of the empathic stuff that Michelle was talking about? How can people talk without words? How can Dad and I hear one another's thoughts? It's as if I was reading his mind and he was reading mine. Words not spoken but sent in energy. Was this similar to faith being like the wind? Could we blow our thoughts to each other without speaking the words out loud?*

Weeks turn into months, all of us on edge thinking that Dad was going to go next. He had been fighting heart disease for **33** years and was now making comments like, "Now, I see why some people don't want to be around anymore." I knew he missed his wife and didn't like life without her by his side. When he would get like this, I'd call the minister for a visit. She always helped him. I never listened to their conversations and oftentimes I wondered what they talked about. I know that through her, he was connecting with God.

During this time of stories and visitors, I adjusted to living with my father. We made plans for his estate, my father receiving advice from my Mom's brother and my Mom's cousin. He wouldn't make any decision without the advice of my Uncle. *Even when Dad was transitioning to spirit, he would need my Uncle's approval that it was ok.* My Uncle was my Dad's connection to my Mother.

It was a cold winter that year and we stayed inside for most of it. My Dad had taken a bad fall the night after my Mother died, so it was difficult for him to get around. I would ask him often if he wanted to go outside for a walk. I knew he wasn't able to, but I liked to joke with him. He would always respond, "I guess not today. Maybe tomorrow." One time I responded, "You always say that. Tomorrow never seems to come." He smiled and said, "I know, that's why I keep saying it."

"Yesterday is history, tomorrow is a mystery, today is a gift of God, which is why we call it the present" ~ Bill Kean

Dad sitting outside in his walker chair.
This would be in April on one of the few
sunny, warm days.

Chapter 9 Unexpected Surprises

"Be miserable. Or motivate yourself. Whatever has to be done, it's always your choice." ~ Wayne Dyer

When I was living with my Dad, we had visitors almost everyday. He loved seeing everyone and it brightened his days. My Uncle and Aunt visited us the most. Dad and I loved it when they stopped in for coffee and donuts. Dad liked to talk with my Mom's brother to get his advice on everything. Dad never had a brother so Uncle David was as close as he would get. I was able to spend time with them; something I hadn't really done since I was young.

The two books that were on top of the coin collection.

One lazy Saturday afternoon, my husband, Dad and I are watching TV in the living room. We were the only ones at the house. Dad says, *"I have a coin collection. I think I know where your Mother and I hid it."* It was like a surprise adventure. He couldn't quite remember the exact location and didn't quite know what would be in the collection. My husband and I look at each other, grin and the search began. We go into the office, where we would uncover the collection in the bottom of the cedar chest. Before we actually get to the coin collection, we are distracted by some books located on top of the coins. Much to everyone's surprise, I pull out two books about sex- one a basic chapter how-to book and one a black and white picture book with drawings. Copyright about 1941.

We all burst out in laughter as my dad clutches his forehead, puts his head down and avoids eye contact with me. I don't usually talk about sex with my father. Although years ago, when my father had a massive heart attack and almost died, he and I watched a movie together at the hospital. The topic was about life after a heart attack. There was a sex part and I was about 13 at the time. We were both silent and then I remember my dad saying, *"Well, I didn't know this was going to be in here."* I think he was thinking the same thing when we discovered books about sex instead of the coins he was envisioning.

The discovery of the sex books would only be revealed to certain visitors when Dad gave me the cue- a smirk and a wink. I would go get the books. I would never say a word unless I got the cue from Dad. We had some good laughs with some of his visitors. So, if you were one of those visitors, consider yourself lucky. When we found them, I assumed the books belonged to my parents. One can only imagine how surprised I was when he shared with a visitor that the books actually belonged to his mother, my Grandmother. *"Oh dear!" I thought, as my Grandmother often said. My Grandmother even had notes on certain pages in the book. Thoughts of my worries about my other Grandmother watching me when I was first married flash across my mind. Well, I guess people have been having sex for a long time.*

After the initial laughter about the book discovery, we did uncover some containers with coins.

While I am writing, fear takes over me. I only have 2 days left of vacation. Can I really write a book in a week? Can I heal from the inside as Anita suggests? Am I writing this to share and, what if I share it, but am told it isn't good enough for a book? I have been writing since Sunday; today is Thursday. I don't want to do anything but write; even though we are on a beautiful beach on the ocean. "Stay present in the now," Eckart Tolle speaks to me. Feel where your feet are, hear the birds, the traffic, the slam of the door. My heart beats faster as I think there is no way I can tell the entire dime story in the next two days. But I want to. I speak to my fear and admit it will be ok if the story isn't finished in a week. Who writes a book in a week anyway? Signs from above take time. I now understand when writers talk about being driven to write. The words come and I don't want to stop. My faith pushing me forward, becoming stronger than my fear. I do know that when this book becomes a movie, it will have to be a musical because of all the Christian songs that guided me during my writing. My story is inspiring.

I remember when I bought my first Christian CD. It was a TV commercial where you could call the number to buy the CD. I called and ordered it, something I never usually did. The CD was called, I Can Only Imagine. Of course, this was long before the internet or Amazon. I remember another song on the CD was a song that my sons sung at the religious school they attended when they were young. It was about our God being an awesome God. These songs I sang over and over again. I had never listened to such inspiring Christian songs. I had only sung hymns in church. I loved those but these made me feel good inside when I sang them. *An awesome God? Wow, that's pretty awesome!*

I remember the night I went to see the movie, I Can Only Imagine. I didn't cry during the movie but I felt God inside me like when I was in church as a child. I had gone to the evening show with a friend and arrived home around 9:30. I was sitting on the couch chatting with my husband and I got a text message from my son. It was 10:00 by then and he usually didn't text me that late. He shares with me that he and his then fiancée thought Grandpa (my father) had sent a message to them. They had named their new rescue dog, Cooper. When they were in the basement with friends, his fiancée looked up and said, "Shamus, look at your Grandfather's sign from the family auto repair business-

Cooper Tires." I cried. His text was perfect timing. I was so uplifted by the movie that this felt good inside, too. *My son believed in signs from Heaven. I had done my job as a Mother. My son would be able to face anything in his life if he believed in God and knew his angels were always with him. One of his angels was most definitely his Grandfather. He knew parts of the dime story, but he didn't actually know the entire story. Writing this book will help even my sons know the whole dime story.*

I pull out a container of coins and a leather pouch with bills. I have no idea what to do with all of this. *"Are they worth anything?"* I question my father. He has no idea but suggests maybe we should sell everything. I think otherwise. We discover Canadian bills and coins. I learn that some of my father's family came from Canada; a fact I had never known before now. We don't tell anyone about our little scavenger hunt and finding. I begin sorting and documenting the inventory; hiding it when any visitors arrive. I would be sorting the coins on the table and quickly put a tablecloth over them to hide my project. The coin collection overwhelms my father but I continue to try to organize the collection. We invite a coin collector to the house to help us sort out the valuable ones and those that could be *considered worth nothing, basically "a dime a dozen."*

I begin to devise a plan; convincing dad that we should divide the coins between his kids and grandkids. He closes his eyes. The work makes him feel tired and overwhelmed. I begin to see patterns in the numbers. **8** Grandkids **4** kids. 12 of these, **8** of those, **4** of this coin and so on. Everyone's coin collection begins. Over the next few weeks, I begin to show him how I am organizing them. He again throws up his hands and says, "ok, whatever." *These coin collections are going to be amazing, I think. I can't wait to give them to everyone. Even if the coins aren't worth anything, they are so cool to have. The Grandkids will be so excited. Imagine having an 1898 coin given to you by your Grandfather! Now, that is a special coin to keep forever. It isn't worth money, but it sure holds a lot of love.*

While sorting, I suggest buying wooden boxes for the coins and a frame for the silver certificates. We had some oddball items in the collection that were worth a little bit of money. Dad wants to sell those and use the money to purchase the boxes and frames for everyone. Dad is from a generation where he didn't use any money from his savings account for projects like this. He would get the money for his project some other way. The items we sell are a unique $4 Canadian bill, a dime worth $80 and a few other coins. Dad doesn't think anyone should get these because then it would make the collections different. Making sure that everyone had similar collections was important to him. We drove to Burlington, and he went into the coin store to sell a few coins and the Canadian bill. Most of the coins don't have any value; they were neat to have.

The coin collection was one of Dad's projects for me as I was there day in and day out. He began to trust me more and more as I showed him that I was able to keep this secret from others. About the same time, he started asking for a shot of Canadian Club (CC) and ginger ale to help him sleep. After my father's heart attack in 1982, he never drank much because he was always worried that it wasn't good for his heart. After checking with his favorite heart doctor, he was able to enjoy some cocktails, which helped him sleep. Although, I never could get them exactly how he wanted them. One night the CC would be too strong; the next night there was too much ginger ale. We laughed as he gave me that sideways smirk while he complained the drink mixture wasn't quite right. I never said a word to anyone. One time Dad mentioned his evening cocktail to my husband, who had no idea what he was talking about. I looked at Dad and said, "I haven't said a word to anyone, including my husband."

With this new drink at night, he shared with me the story of his father, in the hospital sick with bladder cancer, and struggling to eat. My Grandfather's doctor prescribed him a shot of whisky, something one nurse did not agree with. It helped him eat, which in turn helped him stay alive. My father spoke to the doctor about how this particular nurse had spoken to my Grandfather about his *"prescribed"* shot of alcohol, which in turn caused the doctor to speak to the nurse. My Grandfather would never be bothered again about needing a drink to help him eat.

I did enjoy spending time with my father during this time, but I was always on edge. I was always worried that my father was going to die next. He wasn't able to do much during the day and eventually wouldn't be able to go out much at all. Winter is difficult in Vermont and we had many cold days that winter. The coins gave us something to do during those long days.

"Heaven may speak to us through a loud, disembodied voice outside our head; a quiet inner voice inside our head; a conversation that we 'happen' to overhear; or by hearing music in our minds or over and over again on the radio." ~Doreen Virtue

Was this voice from Spirit within me all the time? Is this why songs continue to play inside my head? Why I hear songs all the time that send me messages? How do I begin to listen? I have so many things I need to change in my life. How will I ever be able to do them all? I need to change the way I eat. I need to change all of my negative thoughts into positive thoughts of gratitude. I need to stop talking negatively about other people. I need to do these things on a daily basis.

"By getting in touch with your true self, you will harness the powers of intuition, insight, imagination, creativity, and intention. These are the qualities of your soul." ~Deepok Chopra

I read Susan Pierce Thompson's book, Bright Line Eating. She talks about changing our habits and how much willpower it takes. She also thinks that flour and sugar are extremely addictive for some people. Her "bright lines" for sugar and flour are similar to my black and white view of alcohol. She believes that she shouldn't have any sugar or flour because they are like drugs. She cites evidence based on scientific research. I have my own research that I did with my own body and I know pain is sending me messages. *Would I be able to follow her food plan- eating three meals a day of whole foods? I tried and I failed. I felt like I needed less sugar from fruit and more protein. I had to have protein to feel good. It grounds me and I am better able to focus. I am more in touch with my intuition as my story unfolds. The more I listen and figure out what works for my body, the better I feel. I had to stop listening to all the advice on the internet and Facebook and decide to listen to my body instead. I need to use the tools I had collected from a lot of experts and just be me. I need to do it my way.*

"To learn to trust my body, I need to tune in to its signals, so I decide to follow a simple approach my father outlines. Before eating, he suggests, practice STOP, for Stop what you're doing; Take a one-minute breathing break, inhaling and exhaling and paying attention to the breath; Observe your hunger, rating it on a scale of one to five, with five being famished; then Proceed with awareness." ~ Mallika Chopra

I had to solve this puzzle. It was imperative if I wanted to be able to enjoy my Grandkids someday. I had to solve this for myself and only I could do it. I had all of the necessary tools. I needed to put them in place. This was real life learning in action. My intuition would tell me that writing about the dimes would help me own my story, admit my imperfections and move forward in my life. This, along with a particular type of dime given by my father, would set me free. God would help me heal through telling my story. Just like the coins being a surprise, I might be surprised to find the answers in the most unlikely places. Just like my parents hadn't told me about the coins, were there other things that they hadn't told me? Did I need to discover the answers for myself?

I remember having a conversation with a friend about how difficult it is to watch your children struggle. We both thought it would be awesome if we were able to share the lessons we had learned during our own struggles so that our children wouldn't have to go through so many tough times in life. *That isn't how life works though. Each person has to learn by growing and accepting our journey. Even someone like Deepok*

Chopra's daughter had to learn it herself. Parents can't do the work for the child. They can only be there to help support them when they need the support.

"Owning our story and loving ourselves through that process is the bravest thing that we will ever do." ~Brene Brown

The coin collections were almost ready to give to everyone, but Dad had one more idea. Those particular dimes. He said, "you know- the ones that are different? They have a different head on them. I think they might be called Liberty Head dimes." Would these dimes help Dad heal his heart? Would these dimes be able to heal me? Would they help me change my internal programming? Would this be my parents helping me find my way in this journey of life? If I was willing and ready to listen, I know the answer is yes. My faith believes that they are here with me helping to write this book, the biggest, unexpected surprise of all.

Chapter 10 A Liberty Head Dime
for Everyone

"Everyone must leave something behind when he dies, my grand-father said. A child or a book or a painting or a house or a wall built or a pair of shoes made. Or a garden planted. Something your hand touched some way so your soul has somewhere to go when you die, and when people look at that tree or that flower you planted, you're there." ~Ray Bradbury

I remember my husband telling me that when the kids were little, he used to walk around the house at night and look in the windows. It gave him a different perspective and made him thankful for his house and family. I tried it recently. I thought of people looking at me from the outside. *What did they see? What would I see if I looked from outside myself? What would I tell myself? From the outside of the house, I can only see parts of the inside, not the whole thing. I think of judging others from the outside looking in. I don't know everyone's story from the inside. I can't see inside the whole person when looking from the outside. Will people look at me differently now that they have seen inside me? I have shown them some of my world from the inside. I think of the two voices inside me and wonder how to treat myself with kindness, no matter if I'm looking from the inside or from the outside. I think of my mother. I really didn't understand who she was and why she was the way she was. Like the coins in my parents' house, I had no idea what my parents hold inside. I had no idea their experiences in life and how those shaped who they were and why they were like that.*

"If you change the way you look at things, the things you look at change."~Wayne Dyer

My family has many of my father's belongings to help us remember him. When we were building my son's new house, we put up my father's flag on the Fourth of July. The flag was the last item that we removed from my Dad's house. These physical things help make it feel like he is nearby. Both of my sons have several signs from the family business. Cooper tires. Goodyear. Raybestos Breaks. *And of course, we all have our dimes.*

One afternoon, as Dad awakened from his nap in his recliner, he says, "*I have an idea for those dimes that are different than a regular dime.*" Ok, I reply. I am curious to see what he wants to do with the dimes. He went on to explain that he wanted to take the Liberty Head dimes and put them in a necklace for everyone."Could we do that?" he asks. I assure him that we can figure it out. My brother's girlfriend made jewelry and was so excited about the project. She and I agree that everyone will treasure their new dime from my dad.

Plans were put into place. We ordered the dime holders and chains. I continued to work on the coin collections and eventually everyone (my siblings and all of Dad's grandkids) would receive their dime necklace and personal coin collection from Dad. *The dimes from my father have only begun, I think as I write. I had no idea at the time how much this one dime from my Dad would mean to all of us.*

I walk down to the beach after taking a few minutes to do Yoga; taking care of my physical body. *I wonder- can I heal my physical pain through writing about my experiences, my connection with spirit? I hear many different voices in my head all saying, "YES!YES! You can and you will!" It's like I have cheerleaders inside me.* My acupuncturist says digestion is sometimes about digesting information. When too much information is given, our body has difficulty digesting it all. I think she is referring to my Master's work in Education and losing both of my parents in a short amount of time. In the past 4 years, I had received my Master's degree in Education, along with my administrator's license. I had lost both of my parents and was the executor of their estate, which included cleaning out and selling three properties. I had learned so much about myself, but I knew there was more to learn. *But was she also suggesting that my gut was directly in contact with my brain? Weren't they two different parts of my body? When I go see a brain doctor, they don't talk about my gut. And when I go see someone for digestive issues, they don't ask me questions about my brain. How were these two things related?*

I feel my mom is even cheering me on. I wonder how this all works. Was she sending me messages to listen to the positive voice inside me? The one that comes from someplace else?

While caring for my parents, I was raising two boys through the ages of 18-21, not exactly an easy task. I wanted to be there to support their transition to adulthood. I wanted their experience to be different than my experience. I wanted them to know I loved them more than anything. I knew they were testing their independence but I also knew they still needed me. When my kids were at this age, I would place myself in the kitchen or living room during that "in between" time. For those that understand this age group, there is this time period when they come home, shower and then head out to see their friends. This is the time you see them the most during this stage in their life. Before my Mom died, I would try to make sure I was in the house at that time as much as possible. Boys are different than girls, or at least my boys were. They didn't talk as often as I think girls do. I could sometimes tell when something might be bothering them. Sometimes I would ask, "what's up?" or sometimes I would be there in case they wanted to talk. When I had this sixth sense, and I was home in the kitchen, they would open up about something that was bothering them. We had some nice heart to heart conversations about a lot of things in life. Although they had some life challenges during this time, my husband and I were there to help them get through it. *They also knew that I believed God would help them and we loved them unconditionally.*

I wondered what my boys thought of me. Was I a good Mom to them? Would they hold resentments about some of my mistakes I had made as a mother? I had most definitely done some things as a mother that I wasn't proud of. Raising kids is hard. I think of how life has changed since I was a young mother. Now, with the internet we have so much more information. I had no idea how to be a good mother. I knew that I loved those two boys and that's all that mattered. I wonder what it was like to be a mother in the 60's or 70's, like my mom. I'm sure life must have been really different then too. Did my mother do the best she could with what she had been given? Just like me? Would life be different for my kids when they became parents? Would each generation change and grow more and more?

"When you judge another, you do not define them, you define yourself." ~Wayne Dyer.

Was I a reflection of my mother or was she a reflection of me? Had she passed on her own insecurities? Had I absorbed them somehow? Again, there was no way to determine this. I would never know her internal voice. I only know my own.

"Who tells you who you are?"~William Sloane Coffin

One time a medium I met with explained that life can be played in a variety of ways. She asked if I thought I was in the *'game of life'.* I wasn't clear what exactly she was asking. I thought I was in the game. *I mean, I wasn't dead so I must be living life as life was meant to be lived, right?* She then proceeded to help me envision a baseball stadium. Where was I in the stadium? *I said, "I was watching the game."* Yup- during my life I was only watching the game. I wasn't involved in the tough at bats with some curveballs being thrown at me.. Sometimes I would watch from the sidelines, cheering others on. When it got hard on the field, I would jump to the highest part of the stadium to watch from far away. When I was younger, I jumped out of the stadium with alcohol. *She told me I had to be all in if I was going to grow my soul. I remember thinking, ugh- that sounds too hard. Visions of wanting to hit the tree with my car in college seemed so much easier than being in the game. Would she think writing this book was me in the game, playing my hardest? I sure thought so...This was hard. I felt like I was being called by God to keep at it. Would I be successful? I hoped I would be but I had to have lots of falls. Brene Brown calls them facedown moments in her book Rising Strong.*

My mind continues to race. The thoughts unending. As I hear children on the beach, I wonder if I will ever finish this story. I know the answer. Life is a continuing journey that never ends. The words keep coming and it is difficult to turn off, as I try to let go, taking breaks throughout my days at the ocean. My head hurts but I continue to write my story. Will the story make sense? I have taken so many detours along the way. Will someone pick it apart- like my college essay so many years ago? Tell me things don't make sense. Suggest putting this here and that there. I don't want anyone to change my story. As I continue to write, I know this is the journey I am meant to be on. I know that through this I will heal. I also know that this is **my** *story. I will need help but will listen to my intuition the entire way and "Thy will be done."*

You can't trick God. I listened to Anita's book Dying to be Me and read Louise Hay's book, You Can Heal Yourself. I tried to tell God that I loved myself. This way, he might heal me. It didn't work. I prayed and the more I tried to convince Him of this lie, the more pain I was in. I told him this so that either 1. It would be true (oh, how I wished for this!) or 2. He would believe me eventually (and I would be healed from my pain). Neither of these happened. My pain would endure. I needed to face my insecurities; healing them through writing. Many years ago, in pain from back surgery, I was first introduced to Louise Hay- You Can Heal Yourself. I have tried her first activity in the book. Look at yourself directly in the mirror and say to yourself, "I love you." Do you know how difficult this is? Try it! I remember thinking it was as stupid as dreaming. Until I can do this with truth, God/Spirit/the Universe will not believe me. I am trying this again and I still struggle with it. I try to look past my skin, and speak to my soul. God will know when I am actually telling the truth. When this happens, I will feel God inside me and I think He will heal me.

Part of the problem is that when I attempt to love myself, I feel like I am being selfish. I worry that people might judge me. I worry that it might seem like I am egotistical. *Why do I think this? Do others feel this way too? I wouldn't want other people to treat me without love, so why wouldn't I treat myself with love and kindness?* I remember when I was a teacher I told students that I might send them to the principal if a student said a put-down to himself or herself. They looked at me funny and said, "Why?" I responded that I don't let anyone treat any of my students poorly. *They thought it was ok if they weren't talking to someone else, but that isn't true. I wanted to change their negative self-talk. I knew I needed help with this so I thought maybe others did too. My inner voice seems to be more negative than positive. This needs to change for everyone!*

"Do you not know that your body is the temple of the Holy Spirit Who lives within you, Whom you have received from God? You are not your own...So then, honor God and bring glory to Him in your body." 1Corinthians 6:19-20

I needed to understand that I had let the stress of life affect my body and it was time to open my heart, ask for help and heal.

Brene Brown shares that Rising Strong is,

"The goal of the process is to rise from our falls to overcome our mistakes, facing them is what brings more wisdom and whole heartedness into our lives."

I realize that I don't know my Mom's story. I don't know why she was the way she was. I felt like she taught me how to sweep emotions under the rug. That way if they were hidden, nobody would notice. Instead, what ended up happening was I thought my emotions weren't all that important. She would compare our problems to other's and they seemed to have it far worse than us. She explained that I should be happy for all of the things I had in my life. Sure, I get the gratitude thing, but I also needed to learn how to work through my feelings. Instead of learning to admit my feelings, I would learn to get really good at story telling. When I had problems in my family, I was taught that if I ignored them, eventually they would go away. I was taught how to be "tough" and keep going. Another thing I got really good at was blaming my problems on other people. I didn't have to admit any wrong doing if I had enough of a story to blame someone else. *What made my mother this way? What was her early life like? Did she have two voices inside her like I do? She hadn't ever really shared her feelings. She didn't like to talk about things when she was here and now she was gone. There seemed to be no way for me to find any answers. Had I been too busy looking at the outside of my mom and forgetting to look inside myself? Were the answers really inside me instead of from my mom?*

While staying with my Dad, we found a photograph of his Mother, my Grandmother. The photo was a tiny one like one gets at a photo booth. My Grandmother was around the age of 20 in the picture. She was talking on an old fashioned phone. Her middle finger was positioned in a certain way. *Was my Grandmother giving the camera the middle finger, just like my Dad did when I needed to draw his blood? It sure looked like it!* We laughed often at that picture during those months. The symbolism of the phone suddenly makes me think- *Was this a way for my Grandmother to send a message to me that she is using some sort of spirit communication system? Did she teach my father how to use it? Was she trying to call us this entire time? Was she calling me now? I was ready to pick up the phone and listen.*

My Grandmother (my Father's mother) talking on the telephone. She was probably about 20 years old.

Dad starts giving the coin collections to everyone. We document everything in the boxes and frames. Silver dollars- not worth anything but cool to have, a variety of quarters, and 1898 (the year my Grandmother was born) half pennies from Canada. The collections for everyone all similar. A little

My Dad with both of his parents.

note is attached to each collection, documenting the coins and a note with love from your Father/Grandfather. The dime necklaces are a hit; Dad wears his to church the first day he attends since my Mother's passing. Greeted by so many people in church, he is overcome with emotions. Mom was always by his side at church. Now life was different with her not there.

Did wearing that dime help him face going to church without his wife by his side? Can an object like that actually have power? Was she sitting in church with him that day? Was that the breeze we felt that day?

I started wearing my dime necklace every day and it helped me to ask God for guidance during this difficult time in my life. It wasn't like I wasn't praying before, but for some reason, this dime made me feel more connected to God and my intuition. From the outside, I had a dime that I wore around my neck, but I felt something on the inside when I wore it. To others, it would only be a necklace. To me, it was so much more. This wasn't any old dime. This was a DIME because it had been given to me from my father. For my kids, it was a DIME because it was given to them from their Grandfather, with the same love God gives to all.

My Dad before he went to church. He is
wearing his dime necklace.

11

Chapter 11 Thy Will Be Done: A Summer on the Lake

In my life, I have to pray to God a lot. When I was young, I talked to God about my emotions and problems. Then, as an adult, I consulted with Him about life decisions. I clearly remember one conversation with Him at Caspian Lake in Greensboro. I had graduated from college and was searching for the perfect job to begin my teaching career. I was twenty one years old, about to get married and I knew I needed some help. I had several interviews and, by the time I got to the Greensboro interview, I was exhausted from the stress.

The afternoon of my interview I drove to the beach at Caspian Lake. It was the first time I had ever been there and I thought the lake was beautiful. I parked my car and looked out at the lake. The water seemed to calm my whole body. The sun was setting and shining on the lake. I wondered if this was where I was meant to be. Then I said a very different prayer. I asked God to put me where He thought I belonged. I asked him to guide me in my decision. Then I drove to my interview at Lakeview Union Elementary School.

The interview in Greensboro was the only interview where I intentionally asked God to, "place me where He thought I should be." The other interview conversations with God that I had were more like,

"Please let me get this job." These prayers were more like wishing on a star. There is a big difference in asking for what we think we want or need versus asking for His will to be done. *This one decision would determine so much of my life. It would determine our family friendships, the neighborhood where our children would grow up, my education career and so much more. I taught at Lakeview for 24 years. I loved all of the kids and their families over the years. When I changed jobs later to teach at the local high school, I even started teaching my second generation! Looking back, I know God placed me exactly where I needed to be. Just like he brought my husband to me at the right time in my life, he brought my husband and I to Greensboro and East Hardwick, Vermont so we could raise our family here.*

"The goal of the rumble is to get honest about the stories we're making up about our struggles, to revisit, challenge, and reality-check these narratives as we dig into topics such as boundaries, shame, blame, resentment, heartbreak, generosity, and forgiveness."
~Brene Brown

The first night that I didn't stay with Dad, he takes a fall. *"Don't tell Monica,"* Dad instructs my brother, who is staying with him. Dad didn't want to "bother me". An hour later, *"you better call Monica"* he tells my brother. His stay in the hospital gives me a reprieve from caretaking. I realize that I can't keep doing this. It's too much for me. Eldon had warned me of this the first week after my mother's death. He said taking care of someone takes a lot out of a person. I knew eventually this time would come. It was here. *I asked God for guidance.* I knew my father didn't want to go into a nursing home but I knew that I could not keep going at this pace. I went back to teaching full time and trying to care for my father nights and weekends. This was an impossible task for anyone. Often times, I would be called away from school with something that my father needed me to help him with. Immediately after school dismissal, I would drive to Dad's house to care for him. Other people did try to help. *I didn't know what to do, but I knew that I had to do something. Decisions needed to be made, and Dad would begin to discover the changes in his life were actually better than any of us anticipated.*

It wasn't easy breaking the news to my father. Basically, he had two options- 1. Nursing home (which he did not want to do) or 2. Hire full time care. I took a day off from school to meet with Dad, his minister, the social worker and a hospice nurse to discuss our options. Dad decides that it is ok to admit him into the Hospice program, not an easy decision for sure. Dad never showed any signs of dementia or other failings so he was able to talk about everything with the social worker. I had brought Dad to all of his doctor's appointments and had been hearing the doctor talk about shutting off his defibrillator for months. For my siblings, this would be the first time they heard about this idea. Shutting off his defibrillator would be part of being under hospice care. It meant that we were not going to be doing any more 'life saving techniques' to save Dad's life. Dad had been fighting to stay alive as he had heart issues for about **33** years. It was difficult for all of us to let that fight go. Dad was proud of that defibrillator. He had to have the batteries replaced. Most people who had a defibrillator didn't live that long. The doctor explained that his heart was extremely weak (like pumping at about 15%) and if the defibrillator did try to restart his heart, it would be excruciating pain for Dad and most likely would not save his life for very long. *His heart was too weak. I wonder beyond the physical pain and problems with his heart, what were the emotions that created this disease for him? For him, he truly thought his engine would be able to be fixed by the medical doctors, the mechanics of our bodies. My Dad always trusted them. The doctors were telling us otherwise. He was not immortal and years of heart problems had led him to this point. The medical doctors could only do so much.*

Being an empath, I had learned, meant that I was able to feel what others were feeling. I had looked up the definition:

"A person thought to have the ability to perceive or experience the emotional state of another individual. *'He was also something* *of an empath, intuitively alert, it would seem, to what was going on behind those faces" (Roberta Smith)' (retrieved from http://www.yourdictionary.com/empath)*

Had my father's heart taken on some of the pain of others? Was being an empath how my father and I were able to send telepathic messages? I looked back at all of the parts of my life when I had tried to help others. Was it because I felt their pain so deeply? Had I taken on their hurts into my physical body? I remember back to the Up With People concert from when I was young. I remember thinking that I had absorbed so much positive energy... was this what being an empath meant? I could "feel" others, both good and bad? I knew that accepting this gift from God would have to be part of my healing. Along with gifts, I would also begin to learn that being an empath affected my food choices, my thoughts, my weight...everything I had struggled with my entire life.

I felt the pain my father had as he was facing death. I felt that his fear was sometimes stronger than his faith. He seemed to have doubts about Heaven. He wanted to know how it worked before he had to go there. Just like Reiki, his questions would go unanswered. He would have to wait to see for himself. *He would need to believe in God. I couldn't help him. This was his journey. He had to be in the stadium for this game.*

We hired around the clock care to begin. For me, this would mean I could be his daughter again, not his caretaker, planner, cook, etc. I would be able to visit and help him with this huge transition. He was happy to be able to stay home but so nervous about all of these new people in his home. He had difficulty remembering everything. He thought these people weren't going to know what to do or let him do what he wanted. He struggled to understand how it would all work. Little did he know, that some of these people would be able to comfort him since he was still grieving. He didn't know that he would make so many new friends. He got to share about his life and got to know them during their long nights of conversation. God had answered our prayers. These people, who my family cannot thank enough, thank me for sharing my Dad with them. They miss him dearly and believe that he is always around. *When I share parts of my dime story with these people, there is no question that he is here with us.*

When I was in the third grade, a fourth grade girl followed me into the bathroom. She peeked over the bathroom stall and began talking to me as I was peeing. I was so embarrassed that someone was watching me pee. She began talking about another girl and how much she hated her. I joined in with her, agreeing with every bad thing she said about the other girl. This was what I had learned from an early age. I believed this girl and I would most likely be best friends because she and I hated the other girl. That's what happened with my Mom and I when we talked about others. We bonded. My brain had been conditioned to believe this and I had been programmed like the child who automatically looks both directions when crossing the street. It was a part of me, like a habit.

When I walked out of the stall, the other girl was standing right in front of me. I had been framed and had no idea. The other girl slapped me across the face hard. I'm sure she also said something to me, but that part I don't remember. This memory is very clear to me. Did I go tell a teacher? Absolutely not. I had been the one who did the wrong thing. I had gotten what I deserved. I shouldn't have been talking about that girl and agreeing with the person. She wasn't a bad person. The only reason I did it was to bond with the other girl. *Is this happening nowadays? You bet. All over the internet. It is so much easier to talk about people on a computer than face to face. Things are written on the computer that people would never say in person.*

Why is this important? Because it is difficult to change the neural connections in my brain. It takes a long time. For me, because this has always been a part of my memory, anytime I start talking bad about someone, I get a sick feeling like they are right behind me, ready to slap me across the face. *Has this happened since then? Yes, Well, not the slap, but getting caught? Absolutely!*

Brene Brown explains that humans love to tell stories. Part of the reason that we tell stories, she explains, is that after telling the beginning, middle and end of a story, our bodies release dopamine. We were built to tell stories, especially emotional ones. *Is this why I agreed with the girl in the bathroom?* The only problem was, I learned at a young age to share stories where I would try to convince others that I was good and the other people sucked. I was taught that I could bond with my mother and others better if I told a story about how awful another person was. I wouldn't admit how I was hurt. By telling a person my side of the story, I felt closer to them and they would be on "my side" instead of the "bad person's" side. I would turn them against the other person. I was really good at avoiding my feelings and being pissed off at others.

"Almost everyone that I have known or have interviewed will say that it's always easier to be pissed off than to be hurt or scared." **~Brene Brown.**

As I slowly began to make changes in my life I found myself getting ill when I started talking badly about others. Making life changes can be a slow process, but I tried to admit the way a situation made me feel instead of always trying to blame the other person for my problems. I was good at fabricating the story to make sure I looked good. I learned that by talking badly about someone, it would make me feel better than someone else. *When I was a kid I never really thought much about it because it would make me feel like I was closer to my mom. Now I see how it divided us all. Instead of being angry with the person, I now try to admit that what they did hurt me.*

I tried to be more like my Grandmother- looking for the positive instead of the negative. I have to admit this is hard stuff. I wasn't perfect but I was beginning to make the changes that would hopefully last a lifetime. I had to override the negative voice and make the voice from God bolder and louder.

I often share parts of my dime story (as I have come to call it) with others; at work, on Facebook, with friends. But, there is so much to the whole story; I can never tell the entire story. I can't start with the secret stash of coins, the necklace from my father and make it to all of the different pieces and parts of the story. *This is not just a story about a few dimes.* It's about faith, connecting to spirits, healing through emotions, loving one's self, finding myself and so much more. *Would sharing my story of finding myself help others? How can one believe in all of these things? How can we prove what is happening? How can we prove that it is a sign?* My Dad once said, (while sitting outside on the deck at camp), "How do you think it all works? Who is 'turning the knobs up there'? I think about someone and then they drive by. How can that work?" Dad wanted to believe that something bigger than us was helping everyone here on earth. *Is my Dad suggesting that God is turning the knobs- making all of what we call 'synchronicities' and 'coincidences' happen? He discovered it after he transitioned to spirit. I notice the word "coin" in the word coincidence again. Was that a sign or some weird thing that I shouldn't even think about? I mean, my entire story is based on coins and coincidences.*

Squire Rushnell calls them "God winks"-

"You're about to confirm something you have suspected all along: that coincidence-God Winks- are little messages to you on your journey through life, nudging you along the grand path that has been designed especially for you." ~Squire Rushnell

About the time we started around the clock care for my father, my mother showed up in a dream. I was worried about leaving my father to attend my niece's wedding. I would be gone for about 5 days. After four months of caring night and day for my father, how could I possibly leave him with his new caregivers? In my dream, my Mother and I were at a wedding and I couldn't find my father. I desperately wanted a picture with my father. My Mother appeared in the dream, wrapping me in a hug (which was NOT normal for my mother!) and said, *"Your father can't make the wedding. He will be fine." Was this a message from my mother telling me it was ok to leave Dad behind with his new caregivers? He was so afraid of the changes. How could I go away for 5 days when he was just beginning to get to know his caretakers? My Mother had spoken to me in a dream? How could she? She was so much younger than I remember her. She had laughed at me when I told her that in the dream.*

She laughed and said, "Everyone is young here." How could this be? How do I believe when she never once showed signs of faith? Was she telling me to believe now? Was she supporting me in my life, making up for all the years I didn't feel supported?

"Picture your brain forming new connections as you meet the challenge and learn. Keep on going." ~Carol Dweck

My brain was beginning to change and believe that my Mother had not only changed, but she was helping me now more than ever before.

I went to the wedding and Dad called to tell me that I knew two of his new caretakers. Their children had been in my class years ago. *Can you believe it? I thought. What are the chances? It had been more than 20 years since I had their children in my class. And now these people were helping me with my father. I had come full circle with these people. First, me caring for their children and now they were helping to care for my father. Had God helped "turn the knobs" to bring these people back in my life to help me in one of the most difficult things I had ever been through?*

We moved Dad to his camp on Lake Elmore in early June. He had mixed emotions about this but, in the end, was happy that he was able to stay there for the summer. When I would visit, he would obsess about a variety of things. He would say things like, "I think there is an animal in the ceiling. There is a stain and I think the animal died and is still in the attic space. I have to move home." We would look and couldn't find anything. Another thing would then become the focus. "I don't think the caretakers want to stay at camp. We should move back home." Every single caretaker would share with me how happy they were to be taking care of my father on the lake. "My chair isn't the right height. I need someone to build it up so I can get in and out of it better." This was something we were able to fix for him. There were some things we were able to help him with, but sometimes it was something he had to work through.

All in all, it was a great summer at camp. We celebrated my sons' birthdays with lobster. Since their birthdays are both in July, we always celebrated at camp each year. This night would be the last time I took pictures of my Dad with my sons. I can't remember all the jokes that night, but it sure was fun to see my sons with their Grandfather.

Merrilee and my Dad on the pontoon boat.

My Dad got to take his favorite caretaker, Merrilee, out for her first boat ride on a pontoon boat. The cat spent one night at the house and then joined him at camp. She was so therapeutic for him! Many nights spent looking at the lake, with the cat in his lap, reminiscing about all of the memories over the years

I stop writing to swim in the ocean, dance around the stingrays, realizing I have been writing for about five hours, only stopping to drink and eat very little. I usually read during my vacation. I even brought five books. Once I opened the door to write, the messages kept coming. I'm digesting all of the great spiritual teachers as I'm learning how to digest food differently. Susan Pierce Thompson teaches that we should eat without multi-tasking. Even though my mind continues to want to pick up the journal and pen- I refuse. I need to eat with intention- asking the food to nourish and heal my body. My beliefs about food are changing slowly. Food needs to nourish my soul. Anita says it does not matter what we eat, we have to love ourselves and feel God within us to be healed from any disease. I feel my gut begin to listen.

"...you may be among those who have experienced the tremendous frustration of trying to explain to doctors that your pain is real and it is persisting, even though all your tests come back negative, that there is no medical explanation for your continued suffering, that surgery should have worked, or something similar." *~ Margaret A. Caudill*

I felt I was now in a similar spot in my life as when I had my back surgery in 1996. I had been to several medical doctors pleading my case that something was wrong. I had to solve this in a different way if I was to be healed. Again, traditional medicine wasn't working. What alternative methods would help me? Would writing be able to heal me? Would unraveling my story help remove the physical and emotional pain from my body? Would it be like peeling an onion? Each layer being removed with the story unfolding? Until there was only the inner core of the onion, like my soul? Would I find my soul through writing and sharing my story?

"Change happens when the discomfort of the familiar outweighs the fear of the unknown." ~ Louie Schwartzberg and MJRaval.

I had to feel the discomfort first. It would take me a long time to look for other ways to find peace. I think this book is the answer, but the dimes would lead the way.

When I return home after my vacation, I have several appointments with healers whom I hope will be able to help me. Unlike traditional doctors, one will do a past life regression therapy, combined with EFT (Emotional Freedom Technique) and the other is a naturopathic doctor. I hope they will be able to help me. I know that I will need to unpack my emotions in order to heal. I will need to change the way my brain is wired. I know what I need to do, now I need to take action and do it. Easier said than done. Tomorrow needs to be today.

My husband and I on top of a mountain in North Carolina. We spent our twenty-fifth wedding anniversary hiking in North Carolina and Tennessee. I called my Dad whenever I was on top of a mountain.

I remember that summer at camp with Dad. I climbed lots of mountains that year and called my father every time I reached the top of a mountain. *Things can change so much from even a decade ago. As a child, I never would have thought it was possible to talk to someone from on top of a mountain. Communication systems. I wonder what they will be like in another ten years.*

I often climbed Elmore Mountain (directly across the lake from camp). When I hiked Elmore Mountain, I would sit on a rock and say, "Dad, wave to me! I'm on top of the mountain." He would tell me he was waving and he could see me up there. I would look down at the camp, where I spent most of my childhood. I hiked first thing in the morning and then stopped in for coffee to check on him. *Dad loved to pretend to wave to me. I loved being able to talk to my Dad on top of a mountain. Calling my father from the top of a mountain would not have been possible ten years ago. People might have laughed at such a thought. What communication systems would we have in another ten years? Will we be able to talk to people in Heaven easily? I felt connected to him as I prayed for his health.*

I spent a few precious nights at camp with him. Waking up on the lake is one of my favorite things in this life. I wake up early and drink my coffee out on the porch. As I look out at the lake in the morning, it was as smooth as glass. Calm and clear first thing in the morning before any boats, wind or people disturb the water. I remember back to my childhood, taking a bath in the lake with Ivory soap (because it floats!) and begging Dad to take us skiing before the wind made ripples in the lake. I wanted to have a smooth ski before anyone else made waves on the lake. I see myself playing out on the raft with my cousins and friends. We played on a rectangular raft. It wasn't the usual raft; it was about a foot wide all around the perimeter of the rectangle. There was a large hole in the middle. We would run around it, sometimes sinking it on one side. Little did I know that this raft was actually a raft from World War II; there used to be a net in the middle. *Was life like that? We didn't really know and understand things until we were adults? Would my memories from growing up on the lake always be inside me? Were the outer edges of my life solid and a net in the middle to catch me if and when I needed it? Was God my safety net?* I enjoy the peace and quiet before the day begins.

The biggest topic of conversation when I visited Dad was what Merrilee was cooking that day. Many people who knew my parents knew that Mom didn't let Dad choose what he wanted to eat. This was one of the things that I wanted Dad to feel like he had some control over. At this stage in his life, he didn't have much independence so I wanted him to be able to feel like some things were in his control. Every caretaker was trained to write a list of all of the food choices that were in the fridge. Then, upon given the list, he would choose a little of this, a lot of that and some of the other things. He really enjoyed his desserts. One of the first days Merrilee was there, she sent me a message- *"Your father wanted a brownie with peanut butter with his coffee this morning. I hope it was ok- I figured he was a grown man and he could decide what he wanted for breakfast. I wasn't going to tell him no!"* And, so it began- Dad ordering lots of desserts and he got to choose to eat whatever he wanted. Many desserts were eaten before his meal. His favorite dessert was the ginger snap cookies made with his mother's recipe.

I think to myself- this is so different than what I am experiencing right now with my food choices. Sugar bothers me. Makes me feel awful. Most people love it but I always feel horrible after I eat it. I begin to choose my treats wisely, depending on how they make me feel. Will I have to go 100% sugar and flour free as Susan Pierce Thompson suggests or will I be able to do more like 90%-10%? Only time will tell. Although Susan feels that sugar and flour cause food addiction (and, for some, it may!), and elimination is the only way to food freedom, I find that I can't do it. I don't want to feel bad if I have a toasted marshmallow (my absolute favorite treat in the world!) at a campfire. Every time I have a negative thought about food, I switch my thinking and bless the food. I am thankful that God has given me such wonderful gifts. One step at a time. One prayer at a time. One meal at a time. I will listen to the voice inside me that helps me love myself as I am.

My husband interrupts my writing. He says, "Are you going to publish that?" I respond, "I have no idea who to share it with." "Maybe you should have been a writer," he suggests. I cringe...What? Me? "Do you know what I am writing about?" I ask. "No," he says.

"It's all focused on the dime story, but it is so much more than that. Everything I have learned over the years. It's so big. I'm not sure anyone will believe in what I am writing about. Look at this," as I fan out the pages of a nearly filled journal. As we talk, I notice a small wire cable above us at the condo. It goes from one balcony all the way across to another side of the condo, crossing over the pool area. It's tiny and it disappears in the sunlight. Sometimes it is visible and sometimes it isn't. I say, "that wasn't there last night." "Yes, it was," laughing as he disagrees. "That cable has been there all the time."

Has my ability to write and listen to my intuition been within me all this time? Were the answers inside me all the time, but I wasn't looking the right way to be able to see them? Like the sunshine blinding the cable, had I let my anger and resentment blind me from seeing myself? I didn't think my ability was there. Just like the wire cable above. The analogy is not lost.

"You must change your focus and begin to think about all the things that are wonderful about You. Look for the positives in You. As you focus on those things, the law of attraction will show you

more great things, the law of attraction will show you more great things about You. You attract what you think about. All you have to do is begin with one prolonged thought of something good about You, and the law of attraction will respond by giving You more like thoughts. **Look for the good things about You. Seek and ye shall find!**" ~Rhonda Byrne

I have been a writer all my life but I didn't see it before? My mind questions myself. I can turn this story into a book. People around the world will hear my story. This book is created with love for everyone.

The words to my favorite song come to my mind. This is the song I want played when I transition to spirit. **Let there be peace on earth by Jill Jackson-Miller and Sy Miller (1955)** I sing the words in my head.

The last picture I have of me with my Dad is from the pontoon boat ride with Merrilee and a neighbor from camp. Dad and I shared lots and lots of camp stories while on that boat ride. We laughed and it was a moment in time I will always treasure.

On the boat ride, my Dad shares that his Grandmother bought our family camp in the 1940's for about $500, along with about 5 building lots directly to the left of the Elmore beach. She bought the lots and then sold them, thinking they weren't worth much. *As I remember him talking about this, I can sense an energy around us. Was that my Great Grandmother? Was it Spirit? Why can't I see anything? Why isn't there proof instead of "just a feeling"? The breeze on the lake is gentle and feels good on my skin as we tour around the lake on the pontoon boat.*

August brought another month where Dad slowly declined.

The voice inside me is still thinking about my husband's casual comment about me being a writer. Processing the possibility excites and scares me at the same time. Is my story good enough? Will anyone want to read it? I remind myself who I am writing for- myself. A voice repeats, "Write, digest the information and it will help you heal." My pen continues to call me. In a hurry, I continue to tell my story. I am reminded of a book I once read, Life's Golden Ticket. It explains that we are all given a ticket to live our life from our soul. The ticket is from the Creator (God). We have to figure out how to use it. In the book, the character reflects on his life so far and the lessons he has learned along the way. I think of my life lessons and where I want my life to go next. How do I want to live? I was finally ready to take a chance, take a risk and speak my truth. The ticket was available to me now and I was ready to use it. My ticket is this book. I need to publish this.

"You can live more fully. You can love more completely. You can make a greater difference." ~ Brendon Burchard

I think about Carol Dweck's growth mindset research. Would I be able to practice what I preached? I tell students all the time that I believe in them. Could I believe in myself and my ability to write? I knew I had to. I had to use that Golden Ticket I had read about years ago. I thought about my own children and other teenagers, most likely struggling with the same two voices inside. *Would this book help them? Would admitting I have anxiety and insecurities help people talk about it more?* I believe it had to. The voice inside giving advice throughout the years, boomerangs back to me. When I think of giving advice to others, it is always a caring, loving voice. I need to talk to myself in that same voice.

"Mindset change is not about picking up a few pointers here and there. It's about seeing things in a new way. When people...change to a growth mindset, they change from a judge-and-be-judged framework to a learn-and-help-learn framework. Their commitment is to growth, and growth takes plenty of time, effort, and mutual support." ~Carol Dweck

Was growth mindset like faith? If I didn't have faith, then I would have a fixed mindset. I would only believe what science was able to prove. I knew there was more to life than what the eyes could see. I had to believe that my faith was stronger than my fear. My faith would lead me in the next journey of my life. Faith was my Golden Ticket. I never would have guessed that this would be my path. I was an educator, not a writer. I had to accept that "Thy will be done" was in God's perfect timing. It wasn't wishing on a star, like how I used to pray. It was accepting the opportunity given to me.

I knew that camp was exactly where Dad needed to be that summer. The lake, the mountain, and the family camp were all a part of him. *He was connected.*

Chapter 12 Transitioning to Spirit

"For change to occur, you must start where you are. Recognize the value of each incremental step instead of just focusing on the outcome you want." ~ Louie Schwartzberg and MJRaval

I remember a conversation I had with someone years prior. She had shared that she felt like she was an orphan because both of her parents had passed away. She went on to explain that it was really weird and she didn't know what to do. I wondered about the word orphan. I always thought of the word orphan to mean a child who had lost their parents somehow. *Wasn't losing my parents as an adult a normal part of life? I understand I will miss them, but isn't that the way the world keeps going on and on? Would I be lost without both of my parents? I had turned into the parent while caring for my dad. I had to organize the household and make sure everything was running smoothly. When did the roles change and what would happen when both of my parents were gone? I don't think I felt like an orphan, but, then again, growing up I didn't think I had much guidance and support. I had been given food, water, shelter, clothes, but I felt like I never got the emotional support I needed. And, if emotions affected my physical body, how was I going to avoid heart disease and all of the other physical problems that could arise? I wonder if the reason people feel like an orphan is because we all feel like a child inside, no matter what our age. Would the child inside me feel like an orphan after my father died?*

I remember the morning well. I phoned camp before I left for work to check to see how Dad's night went. The previous day Dad had a bad cough so I was concerned. Congestive heart failure, like it did with my mother, was affecting my father's breathing. The gentlemen caretaker who answered reported that Dad had an "ok night." It was the same gentleman who was excited a few nights prior that the cat was now sleeping with Dad. I felt that the cat sleeping with him meant he was close to transitioning. I had heard about cats at nursing homes. The cats seemed to visit the people who were about to die. That same night Dad had woken up confused, thinking there was a boy in his bedroom. *I knew intuitively that the young boy was his Grandfather. Of course, there is no proof when I am in touch with energies. It was just a "sense" or a "hunch". I was scared to share that idea with anyone. Who would believe such a crazy idea? But I knew it was true. I felt it. It was in the breeze that summer day.*

Dad had some pretty tough days that summer. He asked a lot of questions, like: "When are all of these people going to stop coming and I just get to live by myself?" or "How much money did all this cost?" or "Who was going to take the boat out of the water?" or "What if the cat gets outside?" He would get stressed and we would call the minister for another visit. This always seemed to help him. Luckily, he believed the cat was his angel, helping him.

I phoned camp at around 7:00 A.M. that morning and was given a reassuring, "all is fine." My gut told me different, but I still went to work. This week was inservice- the teacher prep week before the students would arrive for a new school year. As I walked up the stairs at school, I reminded the principal and guidance counselor that my father was still not well- therefore I might not be able to meet with them about the Math classes they wanted to talk about. They had heard this before, but I knew this time something was different in the way I said it. *I had a feeling.*

Sure enough, about fifteen minutes later, the phone call came through the school landline. Merrilee was frantic. Dad had a coughing spell so bad he couldn't breathe. I could hear the fear in her voice. She had called the hospice nurse but didn't know what to do. As I walked outside to go to my car, a colleague hollers, "Hey- how come you get to leave? That's not fair!" Barely looking up in my haste, I respond, "My dad is not well." *He feels it in my words and sees it in my face.* He instantly apologizes and continued to apologize for months afterwards. He had no way of knowing how ill my father was. I knew he could see the panic in my eyes, unspoken fear being sent through the air.

That day would have been Mom and Dad's 60th anniversary. *Was his heart breaking? Was he ready to be reunited with her? I had heard about things like this happening, but hadn't really put the pieces together, until I was on my way to camp to see my father. This was their anniversary. He missed his wife. His heart was literally breaking.*

I don't remember the drive to camp but my adrenaline kicked in and I began planning. I was in my head, not paying any attention to driving. Oblivious to the road, the cars around me or the houses I pass. I knew the road by heart. I was driving to the place I spent most of my childhood. The nurse would arrive about the same time as I did. *Would we need a hospital bed? Would we need to move Dad back to his house? How bad was he? We had been worrying for almost 8 months. Was it his "time"?*

We pack everything to move Dad back to his house. The last thing we would pack up was Dad. He walks up the hill from camp, using his walker. We lock up the camp and begin the drive to Morrisville. *Just me driving my Dad in his van. What will we talk about? I can sense that he is scared.* He is having difficulty breathing and he is coughing a lot.

One of the projects I asked Merrilee to help dad with was to choose who got some of his furniture. He refused. He told Merrilee,

"My wife said to let them fight about it after we're gone." I wouldn't discover until later, but Merrilee, instead of agreeing with him, (bless her!) responded, "Is that what *you* want to do? What does your heart want to do? What do you **feel** in your heart?" During the drive down to Morrisville, I brought this idea up again. We had just passed the round barn and the *dimes came to my mind.* I explained to my father that a bureau given to you by your father or grandfather was more than just a bureau. Similarly speaking, *"A dime is just a dime, but, a dime from your father or grandfather is a DIME!"* Jackpot. He got it. He understood the importance of giving furniture instead of all of us wondering his wishes and/or fighting like he said my mother suggested. He would make the decision of who got which piece of furniture. **A bureau would be more than a bureau!!** It would be a bureau from your Grandfather. A desk would be more than a desk. It would be a desk from your father.

When we arrived at his house, Merrilee, Dad and I sat in the living room. My father was sitting in my mother's recliner and Merrilee and I were on his couch. Dad had requested "cowboy" beans from the local brewery for lunch. As he tried to eat, we created an organized list of furniture to be given to his kids and grandkids. Dad began to decide piece by piece or set by set. Four antique pieces would go to his four children. When Merilee said a piece or set of furniture, he would say the name. Grandkids were a bit more challenging for him to keep straight, but we managed to write who got what furniture. One of the funniest parts during this time (which was difficult because he was going downhill so fast that day), was when he suggested giving my son the dining room table and chairs. *"Don't you think his 'wife' would like that?"* He repeated this 2 or 3 times. At the time, my son wasn't married. We joke and say that Dad knew he would marry her someday! They got married on **8-18-18**.

Soon after finishing his wishes for the furniture, and signing the paper, he began going downhill fast, barely able to talk without having a coughing fit. All of his Grandchildren and my siblings would come for dinner that night, *everyone understanding that he was most likely transitioning to spirit soon. My family all prayed.*

Most likely he had a stroke in the night. We tried to comfort him as much as we were able and were very thankful when the nurse arrived in the morning. Many people stayed to help us during the next few days. *I had never watched a person die like this before. It was a difficult transition for Dad. Was he stubborn? Scared? I knew he didn't want to leave because he didn't know what Heaven would be like. Maybe it would help if we tried to explain that Heaven wasn't as far away as he thought it was. Would that help him? This initiated the "talk" I would have with my father. I know he was listening but was unable to respond.*

It went something like this:

"Hey dad- there is this new communication system you haven't heard of yet. It's a new Spirit Communication system. It's where angels in heaven can talk to humans on earth. It's awesome and works well. You won't really be away from us. We will be able to talk all the time. I can talk to you and you can talk to me. We will always know that you are here with us. It's kind of like a new telephone system (my dad was a mechanic and always had to understand the details of how things worked). It works so well you will be able to call me anytime and I can call you too! Mom has already tried the new system and she is excited for you to join her. Your Mom is there too! Your Mom is waiting for you." I told him over and over again that his Mom was there and he would be able to talk to us from Heaven. *"You can send messages anytime you want and we will all talk to you too,"* I whispered as he moved his head slightly. *I wondered if he could hear me? If only I had read the book, the first phone call from Heaven by Mitch Albom, I would have added, "the end is not the end."*

Spiritual songs soothed him during his last night and morning. His caretakers, myself and my siblings played Christian songs on the iPad. Those songs helped all of us as we said goodbye to an amazing man. Songs like Amazing Grace soothed him while his body fought the good fight.

Recently, I was shopping at a mall. I remember hearing a conversation between 2 kids as they walked the opposite way I was walking. I only heard a small part but wondered what they might be thinking about. One said, "I wonder what it is like to die." *It made me wonder- was this kid an empath too? Why would they say something like that?* He went on to say something like, "I am not talking about a gross kind of death. But, you know, what will my life be like after I die?" I remembered back to college when I dreamed of leaving earth. *Did young people have a sense of what Heaven was like? Was this kid an empath like me? He seemed to have a sense that there was something beyond this time. What if all of society knew that there was more to being human? Would we cherish each day instead of running around being busy all of the time? Would it slow us down and we could learn to take care of ourselves better? What would Heaven be like for my father? Did he have reason to be scared?*

That Friday morning, my siblings, friends and caretakers all gather around. We had been up for the past two nights, hospice nurses in and out at all times. Dad had made some good friends with the caretakers who we hired to help him over the last few months. A few of them stayed to help us. They had been through this before and knew what to do. I was so grateful for not only their care, but their friendship during this time. We knew my father was close. To me, it wasn't 'death' as many people describe. He was changing his form. He was getting rid of the human, physical body to trade it in for his soul spirit, where he would move on to be with God. *He would become an angel and help us with our human experiences. I wonder if he will be able to connect with us like I promised him. He had 79 good years and was now going to be reunited with the love of his life, my Mom.*

Many messages came to me during those last few hours. I was listening to my intuition and, even though my father was dying, I was trying to only think positive thoughts. *We all knew this was coming. It was even harder to go through. I didn't know how to do this. My mother had left us so quickly. This was so different.*

I got the feeling that he didn't want me by his side. Not knowing if he didn't want me there when he passed, I took a walk out into the kitchen to get a drink. I had heard people say this before- that someone had waited for a person to leave the room before they died. *Was I that person for my Dad? Did he want to do this without me? Did he want to be with someone else for his final moments on earth?*

A thought came to me- I told my brother's girlfriend that I thought Mom wanted her to go talk to Dad. My Mom loved her and thought the world of her. She looked at me and asked, "How do you know that?" I said, "I don't really know. I just feel it and had to tell you." Laughing as I shrug my shoulders. *Was it really a message or was I just making up a story in my head? I didn't know but I did know that the message wouldn't stop until I shared it. Repetitive thoughts....were they a voice from spirit?* She went over to my father while I stepped outside for a moment.

My Uncle, (my mother's brother), was in the driveway. There were so many people around, he hadn't gone into the living room to see my Dad. I spoke right to his face, a voice inside me begging me to speak the words, "Get back in there and tell him it is ok to leave us. He wouldn't do anything all these months since Mom died without your blessing. You are his only connection to Mom. Get back in there and tell him it is ok to leave now. Do you understand me?" He laughs and follows my orders. I stand there not even knowing where those words just came from. These voices inside my head once again guiding me during one of the hardest things I have ever been through in my life. Was this something to do with being an empath? Usually my voices had negative and fearful thoughts. What was this all about? Was I supposed to listen to them?

I go back into the house. We had decided earlier to give Dad some morphine to help him transition. He didn't like morphine normally because it gave him hallucinations. When I spoke with his heart doctor about morphine and dad's concerns, we both agreed that at this point, it would be ok. I return to his side to continue giving him some more morphine. When he was close to transitioning to spirit, he yelled out "MOM!" several times. Because he had had a stroke, it was difficult for him to speak clearly. *But there was no denying what he said when he hollered this. I believe my Grandmother, my father's mother was there welcoming him into another realm.* He breathed his last breaths with many of us standing around his bed. He had listened to my Uncle's advice one last time. His body now empty; his soul continuing on, like a motor that will run forever.

The house empties slowly after they have taken my father away. I stay with him until they take him. After three long days with very little sleep, I go home, blurred by the reality of it all. Both of my parents are gone and the reality of it hits. *So much to do and so little time to grieve. Am I an orphan now? I had been parenting my father for months. I hadn't felt like a child anymore. Now, I felt like I had more angels watching over me.*

That was a Friday, with the first day of school approaching on Monday. I had missed the entire week of teacher prep and inservice. I wanted to be there to greet the students as the first day is always the most exciting day of school. I have time. The funeral is not for another week. Just as the colleague who questioned me walking out of inservice, another colleague innocently says before school starts that morning, "*Good morning! How is your Dad?*" I froze. How do I tell her? Poor thing! "*Well, ummm. He passed away on Friday.*" The reality hitting me as I state it out loud. She feels awful (Sorry!) and I continue to try to make it through the rest of the day. I am so thankful that I worked with such a caring team that year. I was able to walk out of school that week and not have to do sub plans. The team took over my classes which helped me so much. I will never be able to re-pay them for the help they gave me during this time of my life. Only a teacher can understand how important this team was to me. Teaching is not a job where I can be out anytime I want. There always needs to be plans in my absence and the kids miss their teacher. People talk about middle schoolers and how difficult kids this age can be during that stage in their lives. During this time of my life, I had the most caring middle schoolers ever. They helped me through several tough days.

I listen again to Brene Brown, Into the Wilderness. She speaks of divisiveness, trust, boundaries. She makes statements based on data and research. I think of my life, have I actually been collecting research to guide me in my journey? Have all of these messages led me to where I am now? Is my research valid? Does my story have any merit? Will I ever be able to connect with my Dad like I promised him? Will all of this information help me evaluate my life and be able to move forward? Will I be able to find my soul's calling? Will I feel like an orphan now that I lost both of my parents? Why did I have to lose them both within an 8 month period? Was this all part of God's plan? What would I do now?

"There is sadness that the relationship was not as good as you would have liked it to be, plus the sense of loss that there is no longer the opportunity to put it right...If you had a relationship like that, then forgive yourself. You were only one part of that relationship and can't take total responsibility, especially since you were the child, not the responsible adult." ~www.griefandsympathy.com

Had I tried to connect with my father and mother the best that I could? Did it matter anymore? Would they trust me to take care of the estate the best way I could? Would they connect with me using the "Spirit Communication System" I had explained to Dad? Time will tell.

My Dad on my wedding day. Forever he will be smiling and winking.

Chapter 13 The First Call from Heaven

"The living can't speak to the dead." ~Mitch Albom

I absolutely hate conflict of any kind. I always try to make everyone happy and am, at times I think, too kind. I live in a small community where we only have a few restaurants. Recently, my husband and I decided to go out to dinner at the last minute. We walked into one of the restaurants, were seated and then nobody came to ask us for our order. After about 10 minutes, I looked at my husband and said, "How much longer are we going to sit here without service?" He agreed that it was weird that we hadn't been served or even offered drinks yet. The restaurant wasn't very busy and there were three waiters and waitresses just standing and chatting. My husband looks around at the situation and, within 30 seconds of my statement, stands up, and is clearly ready to leave. We walked out of the restaurant and went across the street to another restaurant. We walked in, saw some friends and sat ourselves down at their table to join them for dinner. We didn't even ask. We just plopped ourselves in the booth and started talking. We then ordered our meal and had one of the best nights ever. Although we were friendly with this particular couple, they weren't normally someone we would go to dinner with. This night was significant. It was one of the first times I walked away from something that I felt was negative. What happened was we found something much better. At the end of our dinner, the couple shared with us they were celebrating their 45th wedding anniversary and were very happy that we had joined them. *Interesting to think that we would have missed out on this had we not taken a different path.*

I had decided to take a different path in the woods instead of trying to climb over the rock, making life more difficult. Because I had walked away from what wasn't serving me, (literally not being served at the restaurant) I learned that I needed to walk away from more things in my life. When I chose to do this, I would find love in unexpected places, just like the lovely anniversary dinner we had with friends.

I remember a phone call from someone who I thought was a good friend. She was apologizing to me for being jealous of me losing weight and me having two jobs. *Wait, what? I thought- am I supposed to feel bad about this? I supported her when she was trying to lose weight and I encouraged her to search for her passion in life. Why would she tell me this? My response to her was, "I just want you to be happy." Remember in my childhood? I truly wanted everyone in this world to feel God's love and be happy. I wasn't prepared for what came next. Her reply back to me, "I* ***am*** *happy. I'm happy* **whenI'm not with you.***"*

"Knowing the world 'out there' reflects your reality 'in here.' The people you react to more strongly, whether with love or disgust or hate, are projections of your inner world....Use the mirror of relationships to guide your evolution." ~ Mallika Chopra

Was I unhappy with myself? Was I a reflection of her inner world or was she a reflection of my inner world? Either way, I had to walk away. We had so much history together but I needed people around me who loved me. I needed to protect myself from people who didn't show me love. I needed to choose who I wanted to be around based on what I received in return. I needed to walk away from people who didn't reciprocate my love. That's hard. Especially when you have spent so many years together making family memories. My outer world had to match my inner world.

I was in the ballpark playing the game and I didn't want this to be a part of my game. My intuition told me it was imperative to my soul growth to walk away from this toxic relationship. I needed to choose my friendships by the way they made me feel. Just like food. Take a taste and if doesn't feel right, walk away. I also knew that my inner world needed to include God. If it did, then He would give me the signs I needed to understand how to live better.

"Love your enemies, do good to those who hate you, bless those who curse you, and pray for those who spitefully use you." ~Luke 6:27-28

I have a sign in my bathroom that says, "Do all things with LOVE." It is my guiding star helping me navigate life's journey. As long as I always do things with love, then I know that no matter what others think, I did my best. Life was giving me chances to show that I was in the stadium now. I was playing the game instead of watching and letting the game happen. I was ready to make the plays and protect myself from people who hurt me. I wasn't going to jump out of the game with alcohol or food. I wasn't going to numb my emotions. I was ready to face them. That comment from my "friend" was a gut punch and when I looked back at the relationship, I had been sucker punched for years. The difference now? I wasn't sweeping all of my feelings under the rug. I was facing them head on. And I was deciding to take another path.

Seven days after my father's death, I climb Elmore Mountain by myself; taking the day to grieve. I need to do this before we have to say goodbye to him. I park in the parking lot near the entrance to the trail. A family (a grown couple and their parents) begin to hike at about the same time as me. I feel safe with them around as sometimes I don't like to hike alone. I sense a connection but don't recognize them. I pass them easily, saying hello as I pass. *My mind races. I worry about what I am going to do when I get to the spot where I used to call my dad and ask him to wave to me. I can't call him today. He won't answer the phone. I keep putting one foot in front of the other, asking God for help.*

I think of Cheryl Strayed as she hikes,

"The father's job is to teach his children how to be warriors, to give them the confidence to get on the horse to ride into battle when it's necessary to do so. If you don't get that from your father, you have to teach yourself" ~ Cheryl Strayed

Had my father given me the confidence to be a warrior? What does that look like? Was it now up to me to teach myself, using the lessons I had learned from all of the challenges of growing up in my family?

My cell phone rings and I am reminded of a medium who says that talking to spirit someday will be as easy as speaking into a black box, referring to our cell phones. No cord. No physical connection; But you really can talk to the person on the other side. Kind of like the "Spirit communication system" I had explained to my father. I share the news of my father's passing and the details of the services with my dear friend, Peggy. I cry and tell her that I don't know what to do when I get to the top of the mountain. She says, *"You will know when you get there." Not helpful, I think. Not helpful at all. I like to know what to do. I like predictability. I like to plan my life ahead of time and not leave it to chance.*

Hiking is my thing. I love the woods. I love the way it relaxes me and clears my mind. While I am crying on the phone, the family from before passes me. I know they see me crying. I cannot hide it from them. *It's almost as though they know that today I need someone there.* I finish the conversation and begin hiking again. Soon, I pass the family again. They are all out of breath on the rock stairs in the trail that seem to keep going up and up. Often times, my friends and I joke that the stairs are either stairs to Heaven or Hell- however you wanted to think about them. For me, even though the walk was steep and challenging, they always made me feel good. For some, they felt like hell because there were so dang hard to get up! *I always chose to think of them as stairs to Heaven- they always led me to the top of Elmore mountain, where I feel connected. I also only believe there is Heaven after our human life. There is no hell; only regrets for mistakes one might have made during their lifetime. Souls will get another lifetime to grow.*

I say hi again as I go past them. They say, "go ahead!" Before long, I make it to the rocks, where I used to phone my dad. I sit and cry. *I can't call him. He isn't at his camp down below the mountain.*

The family arrives shortly after and I begin to apologize for crying and ruining their beautiful hike. I explain that my dad died last week and I always used to call him from this spot. I point out our family camp where he would pretend to wave to me. *I think to myself- do they really care? Why do I share so many intimate details with strangers? I could just sit by myself and then head back down the mountain, not sharing my thoughts. Why do I always feel the need to connect with people?*

I find out this is the first time they have ever hiked Elmore Mountain. I share that this is my home where I grew up. My Great Grandparents even used to own the town store! They offer me a hug and I accept, apologizing for being sweaty and smelly. Then, the younger gentleman approaches me and asks, *"Do you have faith?"* I begin to crumble. "Yes, if *you only knew how much!"* I begin crying harder.

"Well, I am a minister. Do you think we could say a prayer together **from your father?"** *This guy has no idea how much this means to me right now. How would I ever be able to explain it to him? How would he ever understand how perfect his timing was? How can I explain about the "Spirit Communication System" I had told my father about? Would anyone else think this was my father's way of calling me? He was using the phone system, where I had said, "It works so well you will be able to call me anytime..."*

I honestly don't remember the prayer because I cried even more. I sobbed loud up on that mountain, because I knew that even though I couldn't call my dad that day, **my dad had called me.** Just like Peggy had said in the phone call, *"You will know what to do when you get there." God was there on that mountain with me, bringing a minister to me, Dad using the Spirit Communication System I had explained to him when he was transitioning. He knew how to use the spirit lines of communication to be able to talk to me. There is no doubt in my mind that he called me that day on the top of the mountain. This wasn't like Mitch Albom's* book, *The first phone call from heaven*, *where I could actually "hear" my father's voice, but I know that God had arranged this minister to be on the mountain that day so that my father would be able to send me a message that he is always with me in spirit.*

I was shaking and sweaty. I didn't know any of these strangers but they had answered my prayer, asking for guidance on the top of the mountain that day. They had helped my Dad phone me. Eldon told me he calls these "*God moments*." *This was only the beginning of those moments.*

I feel God as I write. I can remember that day, holding hands with a stranger on the mountain while he said a prayer. As I write this, my crown chakra is so open that I feel lightheaded and free. I'm sitting near the pool and I have to work to ground myself by looking around me. When I am like this, I feel like I am in two worlds. I feel the energy around me. All of my angels helping me write. To ground myself, I focus on 8 things directly where I am. This helps relieve my anxiety. It helps bring me back to reality.

Dad's funeral was on a hot day and the ceremony was long, fulfilling his wishes with a lively Amazing Grace and a proper farewell from the Free Masons. As I held my family, spoke at the service, listened to the minister tell everyone that Dad believed the cat was his angel, lowered him in the ground with a ginger snap cookie and ate desserts before dinner at the church reception, *I knew that his physical body was gone.* Anita's voice speaks to me, almost like my father is speaking through her,

"That body whose hand you're holding isn't the real me. We'll always be together, connected through all of time and space. Nothing can separate us. Even if I physically die, we'll never be apart. Everything is perfect, just as it is. I know that now, and I want you to know it, too." ~Anita Moorjani

It is difficult to explain what life is like after taking care of someone full time. I had so much time that I didn't know what to do with myself. The estate work would soon begin but I was so used to always being worried about my father's care. My adrenal glands were shot and I found it difficult to relax. My nervous system would take years to recover. I was used to being glued to my cell phone, just in case a call came and something bad had happened to Dad. I was on edge 24-7 and now he was gone. The estate and my school work for my Master's degree took priority for many months. There is so much paperwork to be completed when someone dies. By Thursday of the next week, I was exhausted. I had been attempting to go to school, helping the team teach when I was able. Family dynamics made it a challenging experience for me. *I decided I needed a break. I needed to try to connect with my father, ask for his help with everything I was dealing with. I needed him to help me. I needed to know that what I was doing was ok. I prayed to God to help me.*

Dad's obituary:

"James Howard Palmer died peacefully in his home on August 28, 2015 surrounded by his family and close friends. Jim was born in Morrisville, Vermont on November 28, 1935, the son of Howard and Ruth (Mudgett) Palmer. Jim graduated from Peoples Academy and later Franklin Technical Institute in Boston. He married the love of his life, Deanna Smith, on August 25, 1957. After graduating

Monica Morrissey
September 4, 2015 · iOS · 👥 ▾

Well, I used to call you every time I got to the top of the mountain and tell you to wave to me from camp. Got to the top and couldn't call you but you sure called me. Here with me just now was a family and one of them was a minister and asked if he could pray with me to help me through this tough day. Thank you God for bringing me a little closer to my Dad 🙏💜

My Facebook post from the day my Dad "called me" from Heaven.

from college, he began working for his father at Palmer's Service Station, a business which his father had started in 1933. There, he learned the invaluable art of exceptional customer service and auto repair. Jim enlisted in the Air Force but was honorably discharged for medical reasons. Upon his return, he rejoined the Palmer family garage where he eventually took over the family business as manager and owner...

Jim and Deanna cherished their summers on beautiful Lake Elmore at the Palmer family camp, which was purchased by Jim's Grandmother in 1941. They especially enjoyed hosting Sunday breakfasts, cooking pancakes, eggs and bacon.....oh the many pounds of bacon...over an open fire for 75 plus people! Hosting the Allen Family Reunions was a favorite for everyone. Jim and Deanna made the Palmer family camp feel like home to all who came to visit. Jim worked his entire life to make camp into what it is today. Jim was able to continue to live at camp this entire summer due to his very dedicated caregivers who became like family.

Jim and his wife enjoyed many trips with friends and family, including trips to Puerto Rico, Hawaii, and Rome. Jim treasured the Florida vacations with the Hale & Towle families. Jim and Eldon Towle would make sure to bring their home made syrup when they went on vacation. He loved to be surrounded by his family and friends, often snowmobiling, waterskiing, many hours spent sugaring, and listening to the kids sing along with the player piano.

Community was important to Jim. Throughout the years, Jim served on the school board, select board, Morrisville Rotary, was a founding member of the Morristown Rescue Squad, a member of the Freemasons and was a church officer for the First Congregational Church. Beginning at a young age, with his Mother, Ruth, his church family was an important part of his life.

Jim had many important people in his life. Growing up, he spent many hours with his cousin, David and a good friend of the family, Gloria Wing. While running the business, all of his customers and business associates became his friends. Jim and his good friend, Eldon, solved many of the world's problems while their wives were shopping. Anyone who met Jim, instantly became a good friend.

A heart attack early on in life made it so Jim had to retire sooner than he expected. This opened up the opportunity for Grandkids to come over anytime. For many years, it was Grandpa's Daycare and taxi service.

Each Grandchild held a special place in his heart. His heart attack was actually a blessing for both him and his grandchildren.

Jim loved each and every caregiver that he had over the past four months. They helped him so that he could stay in his home and the camp on Lake Elmore where his friends and family could come and visit him anytime. Jim was very thankful for the care that Merrilee Perrine, Home Health and the company,Love Is, provided. He held a special affection for one particular caregiver, his precious cat, Missy. She was a rescue cat who became his Guardian Angel. "

I realized that since my father had been in the customer service business, I had watched him try to please everyone. The many customers throughout the years loved my parents dearly. Happy customers meant more business, right? What I didn't understand was that it's impossible to make everyone happy and this wasn't my job in life. As I learned about being an empath, I realized that my whole life I had wanted to help everyone. This is why I gave so much advice all the time. Letting that go was going to be so important to my health and well being. *Will my dime story be the way I can help people without making myself sick? Will it help some more than others? Is it worth the risk? Free will and free choice will determine everyone's path. Either choose the one that looks fresh and new or the path that has been stomped on by shoes.*

"Don't try to win over the haters...You are not a jackass whisperer."~Scott Stratten

Chapter 14 The First Dime from Heaven

"The definition of *coincidence* found in the *American Heritage Dictionary* is 'A sequence of events that although accidental seems to have been planned or arranged.' This definition, of course, begs the question, 'Planned or arranged by whom?' Most people will answer, 'By God, that's who.' Whatever you call the creative life force, it seems to be not just an architect of the past but of the very minute-by-minute present of our lives." ~Squire Rushnell

Was Squire describing the same thing my Dad had wondered about when he had questioned, "Who do you think is 'turning the knobs' up there to make all of this work?"

I was lucky that I didn't feel like an orphan after both of my parents were gone. I had Eldon who I started calling Dad as he always felt that I was like another daughter to him. Merrilee, who had taken such good care of my Dad, told me straight out that she loved me so much that she was adopting me. So now, I have people who I call Mom and Dad. I can call them anytime. They are not the traditional parents, but I sure do feel loved. I am also extremely lucky that my Aunt and Uncle became a big part of my life. We had connected after my Mom had died and I enjoyed getting together with them. Through these 4 people, I learned more about my parents. They shared stories when we got together and I am so thankful to have them in my life. I could tell that my Uncle loved his big sister a lot.

It had been exactly two weeks since my father had transitioned to spirit and a week since Dad had "called me" on top of the mountain. I took a day off from work. Before I would tackle the paperwork and phone calls, I hiked Elmore Mountain again. I was determined to take time by myself to clear my head. There was so much to do for the estate and I needed to be able to think. I wouldn't be able to call my father today when I reached the top of Elmore Mountain. He again wouldn't answer. I called him often this summer telling him to wave to me from his camp below on the lake. I hadn't figured out a way to call Heaven yet. I know for sure he called me last time, but what was I going to do today? I couldn't expect another miracle like last time. Last time, Peggy had told me that I would know what to do when I got to the top of the mountain. Today would surely be different.

"But ask the animals and they will teach you, or the birds in the sky, they will tell you; or speak to the earth, and it will teach you, or let the fish in the sea inform you. Which of all these does not know that the hand of the LORD has done this? In his hand is the life of every creature and the breath of all mankind." ~Job 12 7-10

I felt so alone as I climbed the mountain; deep in thought as I walked. I wanted to believe that my Dad was helping me climb the mountain every step of the way. I could feel it in the wind and wondered where the animals in the forest were. It was the end of summer. Soon the leaves would be falling and the snow would blanket the forest.

I made a plan on the last few steps toward the rock where I would sit to call my father. I always knew the last part of the hike was when I would see white birch trees. I remembered this when I was a kid climbing the same trail. I always liked to know when I was almost there. The trees opened up and I could see the sun shining on the white birch trees on either side of the trail.

The dime I found on the top of Elmore Mountain. The year is 1995 and it has a "P" above it. My son, Patrick, was born in 1995.

I decide to phone Merrilee. She always answered anyways. When I phoned her, she and I both agreed that we missed my dad a lot. I paced while on the phone, trying to calm my nerves. As I walked towards the rock where I always sat to call Dad, I couldn't believe my eyes. *How could this be? How does a coin, this particular coin, land on top of the mountain, exactly in this spot? Was my father grinning like this was some sort of game to him? Could he really do things like this from Heaven? Did he leave physical evidence as a sign that would only mean it is from him?*

"Merrilee, you will never believe what I found on the ground, right here." I can't even believe it as I try to put words to what is happening. It feels surreal. I have nobody around me this time on the mountain. She says, "I can't believe it." The rest of the conversation is a blur as I feel my father's energy all around me, enveloping me in the biggest hug I have ever received.

"Your dad knows how you feel, because he's able to read your mind and heart from his vantage point in Heaven." ~Doreen Virtue

A voice whispers to me, " Yes! It is me! I figured out that Spirit Communication System that you whispered in my ear the day before I left my body. You know- where you said I could call you and you could call me anytime? That new spirit phone system. Isn't it great? We really can connect from here. Remember how I called you last week? I didn't have the faith that it would work, but now I know it to be true. You told me my engine would still be running- this engine is so different! I'm not in any pain and I know my engine will run forever."

I was not expecting another sign today. *The last one was so clear but this one? How could it be? I can see my Father grinning, thinking that he really figured out the system I had whispered into his ear, shortly before transitioning. Of course he figured it out- he loved stuff like this!*

If my father had read Mitch Albom's book, the first phone call from heaven, he might have been able to tell me more about heaven. Something like,

"In heaven, we can see you...We can feel you...We know your pain, your tears, but we feel no pain or tears ourselves...There are no bodies here...there is no age...The old who come...are no different than the children...No one feels alone...No one is greater or smaller...We are all in the light...the light is grace...and we are part of...the one great thing." ~Mitch Albom

I pick up the dime and so begins me sharing my dime story with others. I do not even remember walking down the mountain. My thoughts engulf me. I wonder how this could even happen. *How will I be able to explain this to people? They won't know the conversation I had with my father before he passed. They won't know about the minister I met last time, helping my father "call me".*

This verified what I have felt my whole life but never felt confident to let other people know about my connection to Spirit. People get shivers and goosebumps when I tell them about it. **I just know.** Dead pen again! When I write the words "I just know"it is again in ghost letters.

I know that every time I run out of ink, it is a sign from God and my father to continue to write this book, this story, to share with others. He always wanted proof of how this all works, now he is continually sending me messages and signs, giving me the courage to share this with the whole **world....** Really? Three dead pens in a matter of a few days. The words **that** disappear on the page have been, "I just know", "world" and "that" Pretty soon, I will have to really search for a pen as I am running out of pens! I feel a sense of peace as I receive this message to share my **story.**- yes another dead pen. I am using my markers that I color with and slowly, one by one they die on certain words.

"I just know"

"World"

"That"

"Story"

A message. I am open to receiving messages, guiding me in this journey.

I still have that dime that I found on the mountain that summer day. It is now in a necklace that I can wear whenever I want. It will forever remind me that Dad is around- a physical reminder that we can connect with Spirit. As we clean his house and camp, dimes start appearing everywhere. The entire family would begin finding dimes. I remember my husband, while helping clean out the family camp, threw a bunch of dimes at me. It was almost like he was scared of them; like my Dad possessed the coins. *I laugh inside. Angels aren't creepy like ghosts. They are around to help us. If only everyone would believe this.* Cashiers, low on change, would give me all of my change in dimes. 30cents- three dimes 60 cents- 6 dimes. *But, this story is so much more than dimes. The dimes make it real.*

"True self-confidence is "the courage to be open—to welcome change and new ideas regardless of their source... Real self-confidence is not reflected in a title, an expensive suit, a fancy car, or a series of acquisitions. It is reflected in your mindset: your readiness to grow." ~Carol Dweck

Can dimes from my Father in Heaven help me to be ready to change my mindset? Choosing confidence instead of anxiety? Can I turn my negative thoughts into positive thoughts? Can I listen instead to my intuition and the many messages from God? Can I change the patterns and the neuro connections in my brain? It's like trying to make railroad tracks go in a different way. The metal of the tracks making the patterns so strong it is difficult to bend them.

"God Bless the Broken Road that led me straight to you."~ Rascal Flatts

Yes, my whole life I felt I was on a broken road. Now, the road was going to be different. God was inside me helping me heal and showing me signs that I was on the right path. God was sending me messages to write this book to share with the world. If I thought of myself as a messenger helping the world, my fears disappeared. I was on my own shiny new path, determining day by day how to love myself for who I am. My Mother and Father were helping me.

Chapter 15 Messages

"Your winks from God can be something of a riddle, something ironic, or just something triggering a smile and a shake of your head. But, when they happen, *you* know- it's a little message to you." ~Squire Rushnell

Sometimes when I am driving, I can drive and not remember any part of the trip. I seriously keep the car between the lines and don't even notice the other cars in front or behind me. I am either thinking of something from the past, most likely ashamed or feeling bad about something or thinking of something in the future, most likely worrying. People will tell me all the time that they waved to me and I didn't see them. It's like I'm in a different world. This is what my life felt like sometimes. A blur. I was driving, but wasn't paying attention to anyone or anything around me. That's what the next few years after my parents died felt like. I was driving, but not stopping to enjoy life.

I knew my father was with me the entire time I was dealing with his estate. Many times I had to pray for guidance during difficult times, similar to what I did when I was caring for him. When I prayed, it calmed my mind and I knew that I was following his wishes.

My father owned **3** properties. We closed on the last property of my father's estate the day before our now annual vacation to Florida in

April. Most of my responsibilities as executor of the estate were over. By now, I was close to finishing up my Master's degree. For the next year and a half, action research would consume my life. My work was like a scientist doing an experiment. Read, reflect, test, read, reflect, test...repeat. *How do I know if I did it correctly? Who would guide me in this journey? Our professor explained that we needed to trust the process. Our answers would come through our work. Learn through the process. I didn't like that. Along with a plan, I liked to know where I was headed. How could I drive if I didn't know my route?*

I liked to have things completed. Finished. Over with; so I could relax. Was action research like our life? Read, reflect, test? Are we all here to learn lessons in life? How can we know if what we believe is true? How will we know if we have learned the lesson? As I continued my research, I compared action research to life's journey- full of questions and always searching for the answers. The more knowledge we have, the better able to navigate life lessons. How many books had I read about past life regressions, being healthy, loving myself and messages from Heaven? Too many to count! I had to learn to enjoy the journey because there really is no finish line. Life is never done.

One of the books I had to read for college was called, Make Just ONE CHANGE Teach Students to Ask Their Own Questions. Of course, the book was supposed to be for my classroom teaching practice. But what ended up happening was I began to think about all of life's questions. *What was my purpose here? As I turned 50, what was left of my life and how did I want to spend it? What did God have in store for me? Would I be able to plan things or should I let God decide my path? Was my path always going to be predictable or was it going to take different roads that I couldn't even imagine? Writing a book was never something I thought I would do. Teaching, real estate and being a mom and a wife had been my entire life.*

As part of my reflections on the research I was conducting, I learned things that would apply to my life also.

"Time in between does help your thoughts take a different path and that is ok. Reflection helps all learners and researchers. Enjoy the process." ~Monica Morrissey

I realize that in taking the time to write this book my thoughts have taken several paths. I have gained new insight about my gifts and challenges. I have discovered that I am an empath. I have realized that my faith is truly stronger than my fears. I still have many questions, but I am slowly being guided to the answers.

"Who looks outside, dreams; who looks inside, awakes." ~Carl Yung

My younger son and I decide to go to a Red Sox game in the fall the year after my father died. Our neighbor's daughter, Samantha, had died suddenly and we were all in shock. She was 27 years old. She was fine one day and not the next. I had even said hello to her in the grocery store the day before she died. She looked fine. Our family talked about how a life to 100 years old was not promised to everyone. None of us knew how long any of us would be around. We knew our life journey was God's decision

I love to plant sunflowers as they were Sam's favorite flowers. We all miss her smile and happy go lucky spirit.

We weren't going on our annual family trip that year to Boston be-cause my husband was helping my older son and his girlfriend build their new house. With winter coming, they needed to finish up the house. Patrick and I decide that we could go without them. Realizing how short and unpredictable life can be, we decide to go to a Sunday game and take Monday off from work. ***The memories are what stay*** *inside of us when a loved one goes to Heaven.* We decide spending time together at our favorite place in Boston is worth the money and the time.

Patrick and I head to Boston to see Big Papi play one of his last games at Fenway. While he was driving my car, he says, "Hey Mom, your mileage is **5,555** miles. Isn't that cool?" *I wonder if I should share that Spirits or Angels show us they are around through numbers? Would he believe me or just think I was doing more "voo-doo stuff"?* I decide that we have plenty of time to chat in the car and it was a great discussion starter. *I so want my children to understand and have faith in the Spirit Communication System available to everyone.*

"Every thought you think creates your future." ~Louise Hay

I begin to tell Patrick that some people believe that repetitive numbers can be a sign from Heaven. Silence. *Explain more, I think.* My number is sometimes repeating ones. I see them all the time. Often times, I can look at the time and it will be 1:11 or 2:11 or 5:11 and so on. I believe that an angel is around and they are trying to send me a message. His cousin Tyler's number is 8. I share that I see those a lot too. He immediately thinks of his Grandfather, his most current angel. He looks at me with wonder in his eyes. I wish I had access to some books or a website to look up what a 5 means. Then I could help him understand what the message might be about. I know he will never Google such a thing. But the seed has been planted. I have given him something to think about and ponder. *Stay in the moment. Don't think about the past and don't worry about the future. Enjoy the time with your son. My inner voice reminds me of how important this is.* After chatting for several minutes, the subject changes and I wonder if he believes.

"1- Stay positive . Think about and focus upon what you like, not what you dislike, fear or what you are worried about...your thoughts create!...

5- Change is in the air! Call upon your angels to help manifest positive new changes in your life...

11- Honor your intuition, it's right on! Keep your thoughts in alignment with your dreams and intentions for the future, and release any doubt or nervous energy into the light. 11 is a powerful number of dreams, intuitive illumination, and connection with spirit." ~retrieved from https://www.ask-angels.com/spiritual-guidance/angels-and-numbers/

During dinner before the game, Patrick says, " Hey Mom- Guess what time it is?....**5:55**!" *Is he beginning to believe in the power of numbers being a sign from Spirit?* The game continues and we have a great time. Big Papi doesn't bat but we still enjoyed the baseball game. When the game is done, Pat says, "Mom, did you notice all the **5**'s? In the **5**th inning, they scored **5** runs and they won the game by **5**." Patrick automatically thinks it is his Grandfather. I know now that my Father was only beginning to send signs to Patrick. Although we were watching the baseball game at our favorite ballpark, I felt like Patrick and I were also playing the game of life. We were learning how to navigate life with our angels in Heaven cheering us on. Shortly after this trip, Patrick got a new job. After he got the job offer, he said, "Mom, I think Grandpa helped me." *I respond, "of course he did."*

*If the dime on the mountain or the dimes we find throughout the years wasn't enough to make us believe, my father would eventually connect with Patrick for **THE dime** that would make this book possible. As I write, my body heals. Telling my story for me and others gives me a sense of peace. If my story can help one person, then it is worth it. I have surrounded myself with other people's words, but never my own words. Will my words now help me? Daring to share is forever changing my life.*

Patrick and I at the Red Sox game.

Chapter 16 Life Marches on

Messages from Dad through a Medium

"'I am a noticer,' he said. 'I notice things that other people over-look. And you know, most of them are in plain sight.' The old man leaned back on his hands and cocked his head. 'I notice things about situations and people that produce perspective. That's what most folks lack- perspective- a broader view. So I give them that broader view...and it allows them to regroup, take a breath, and begin their lives again.'" ~ Andy Andrews

I had a good collection of tools in both my personal and professional life that I had collected over the years. Books I had read, conferences I had been to and general life lessons learned through some of the more difficult times in my life. I remember taking a group of teachers to a conference. During one of the breaks, a young teacher looked at me and said, "This is such a good conference." I agreed. Then Ryan looked at me again and said, "None of this is new to you, is it?" I smiled. "No, it's not," I said. After 27 years of teaching, I had lots of experience but also didn't quite know how to share the knowledge I had gained over the years.

I had a lot of life experiences too that had helped me grow as a person and a teacher. I had changed so much compared to the person I was during my first year in college.

I was lucky that my Master's program was built with constructivist values. During my studies, I wasn't told what to do and believe, I was encouraged to "find my passion". We read books like, A More Beautiful Question, Make Just One Change, Strategic Inquiry, and Leading with Soul, An Uncommon Journey of Spirit. I wasn't just learning to be an administrator, I was discovering why I wanted to be a leader. I learned to not only think about what great leaders are able to do, but to

"...develop a life and livelihood that center on meaning, purpose, joy, and a sense of contribution to the greater community." ~ Bolman & Deal

Wait, what? I just wanted to finish my Master's program. This wasn't about finding myself. Just complete the work, get the degree and possibly get a new job. Not only did I have to think about why I wanted to lead, but the program forced me to dig deeper into **my** *why- almost like* **why am I here on earth kinda why.** *It was as if they were asking me to think about why God would want me to be a leader? Wait, they were mixing religion with school, weren't they? Can they do that? But it wasn't like organized religion, more like spiritual religion. Can I really think about my educational journey as a spiritual journey too?*

During this time, I discovered Simon Sinek, who wrote the book, Start with Why. Because of my previous readings during my Master's work, I was curious to learn more. *Had I discovered my passion? Was this work inspiring me to peel the onion a little further and get to the deeper understanding and answers to my life's journey?*

"Leadership is not a rank or position to be attained. Leadership is a service to be given."~ Simon Sinek

Was I only getting my Master's degree to "move on up" or was I ready to be a true leader dedicated to the hard work of the people? Was writing this book helping me lead in a whole different way than I imagined? Had

I found my calling? Something that I never saw coming? Is this what God had been planning all along? How would I know?

When I became a Real Estate Agent I learned that teaching and real estate are two very different professions. Well, at least in the sense that the day to day work is very different. One is sort of predictable and the other is not. With teaching, I couldn't predict what the students were going to do, but I could predict my schedule. There was a rhythm to the year. Begin the school year at the end of August, and end the school year in June. Work every weekday for the most part from Monday to Friday, 7:00-4:00ish. I had lunch at the same time every day and I could plan on the day ending around 3:00 for the students, but the planning would never end. It was predictable.

When I started real estate, that was the first thing that I noticed. It was unpredictable. I had to learn to adjust. I would go to the office in the morning with nothing on my schedule, and then all of a sudden have several phone calls and appointments. So many that it would be 4:00 and I had not even eaten my lunch. For a girl who was used to eating at 11:30, whether I was hungry or not, this took some time to adapt. Being a teacher, I could always plan on who my students were for an entire year. For real estate, I had no idea who my clients were going to be and no idea if the deal was going to go through. For real estate, I had to learn that the universe would help make the match for someone to be able to leave one house and go to another at the exact time that someone else would move into the house being sold. There had to be someone behind the scenes guiding the perfect timing. I wouldn't be able to control it. I would be there to help the deal go smoothly, but ultimately the transaction would be out of my control.

In teaching, I was constantly planning. It was my job to make sure every lesson went smoothly and the students got what they needed. I was in control for all of the planning in my classroom. *Was being a realtor supposed to teach me to believe in letting the future unfold instead of trying to control it? Was it forcing me to feel out of control so that I could learn ultimately that God is in control?* I had a difficult time adjusting because real estate was different than teaching in so many ways. *I had to learn to let go of the outcome.*

I grew up thinking that people who believed in such things as mediums, after life and such were not very smart. Well, maybe not that they weren't smart, but the way my mom would roll her eyes sent a message that it was sort of dumb to believe in such "nonsense". As I slowly began learning about a variety of different beliefs, I wondered if I would ever truly believe in some of these things. One medium in particular sure did change the skeptic in me. With organized religion, I felt that God was always there. With Mediums and past life regression work, it was unpredictable and I never knew what was going to happen. *Did I have the guts to take a risk and find out what life might be like when I changed my thinking about these things? Would I believe that God would help me along this new path? Would it challenge me to change my beliefs? Would I ever truly believe?*

A friend of mine was going to a group event. A medium would be speaking in front of a large group. Some people would be "read" and others might not. Being "read" meant that someone from Heaven wanted to send the person on earth a message. The medium would be the messenger. I met Tracy and Chelsea for dinner and then we went to the event. All day long, I had been thinking about my Dad, the dimes, and the mountain. I felt him everywhere. I even found a few dimes and a penny. I prayed that Dad would come through for the event. When we arrived, we sat in the very front row. When I sat down, I sat down next to two other friends, Samantha's Meme and Aunt Ellen. I felt awful. I had been wishing for my father to send messages through the medium but these people were in a lot more pain than I was. It had been over a year since my father had passed and losing a parent was a normal part of life. It had been only a few short months since Samantha had died and it wasn't normal to bury someone so young. *Please, I thought, send a message from Heaven to them instead of a message from my father. I'm sorry for being selfish today. They need this way more than I do.*

The medium was not what people envision when you think of a "typical" medium. I'm actually not sure what people think someone should look like, but according to my mother, they were all "crazy" people. The medium had tattoos, swore like heck, and basically did a comedy act along with her readings from Heaven. At the beginning of the "show", she told us if we didn't like the word fuck, we might want to leave right now. This was not the place to be. The first person I remember her reading was a young woman who had lost her dad. The medium got it right that one of the reasons she was so upset was that she was getting married and her dad wouldn't be able to walk her down the aisle at her wedding. *See, I thought. I was selfish in my wish to have my dad send me messages today. I was able to have my dad walk me down the aisle at my wedding, he got to see my kids grow up and I was almost 50 years old when I lost him.*

Does anyone see a pattern here that I was taught at an early age? I was comparing myself, my loss and my grief to someone else's loss. Mine wasn't "as bad" as the other person's grief or loss. What I had learned when I was young was that my emotions weren't important because they weren't "as bad" as someone else's. Comparatively speaking, *should I not be upset that both of my parents had died? Should I numb my feelings and know that others had it much worse than me so I should be fine? (this is what was programmed in to me at a very young age) We all felt the pain of losing someone we loved and all of our emotions mattered.*

The medium was receiving messages from heaven to the woman sitting directly behind me when, out of the blue, she says, "A dime a dozen." I think of my dime on my neck, grab my necklace, and look up at the medium. She states it again, "A dime a dozen." Her eyes meet mine as she sees me holding my necklace. She walks closer to me and says, "Is that a FUCKING DIME?" In this event, the audience is only allowed to say yes or no because she does not want us giving any more information. I say, "yes," in one of the quietest voices I have ever heard without it being a whisper. She went on to give several bits of accurate information. It went something like this:

"Was your father a jeweler?"

"No." *but it was his idea to make the necklaces. I wasn't able to say this but she was stuck on this idea that he made jewelry for a living. He didn't, but I think he wanted credit for the necklaces being his idea!*

"He had lots of properties. He was proud of those properties. It was almost like he had struck oil in Texas. 3?"

"Yes, 3 properties"

"Why Texas? I see some sort of military uniform."

She allowed me to say more than yes. "He was in the air force and stationed in Texas for basic training."

"He seemed to have rose colored glasses on most of his life. He wanted everything to be good but couldn't quite seem to view life with some of the dysfunction that might have been a part of his life."

"Yes."

"The dimes aren't worth anything though, correct?"

"Yes." *Well, I think. No monetary value, but I wouldn't ever give it away or sell it. This dime is from my father, so it means more to me than money. I wish I could tell her about the dime on the mountain.*

"Well, that makes sense, a dime a dozen!"

She went on with a few other connections but said she had never had a clear message like that with so many meanings attached to it.

She went on to give other messages from Heaven that night. It seemed like I connected with almost every story in the room. One person's sign from Heaven was a four leaf clover. *A message from my Grandmother too?* Another person's sign from Heaven was a rainbow. *When my husband drives and I look out the window at a road sign, if I look just right at night, I can see a rainbow. After my Mom died, I envisioned her saying, "I know it is quick and short, but it is your sign to believe." I have no idea why I thought that, but that is what I would think. I thought it was a sign from my Mom.*

"The pendulum of the mind alternates between sense and nonsense, not between right and wrong."~Carl Jung

I was born in October and I am a Libra sign. Libra, according to the Zodiac signs is represented by a scale, with both sides distributed evenly. This is both a blessing and a curse. I see both sides of everything. I want balance everywhere I look. *Can my beliefs be balanced? Can I believe in mediums, past lives, and healing from God all at the same time? I think back to one foot in the living room where my parents are sitting and one foot ready to leave. Have I always had one foot on earth and one someplace else? Is this part of being an empath? Or is it something else?*

I stop writing to sit by the ocean with my husband. I tell him that I am thankful for his support this week; it means a lot to me. He responds, "I want you to be happy." My reaction is not like the punch in the gut when I told someone the same thing. I cry because I know what he said is true and I accept his love. We go swimming in the ocean, on our last day of vacation.

I went to see a hypnotist who was trained by Brian Weiss. In fact, I have gone to see her several times. I was so scared that I wouldn't be able to relax so that I could find another lifetime, my childhood conditioning so trained to not believe in such things. I was fascinated by all of Weiss's books, where people were healed through a past life regression therapy session. I decided to try it. In one of the lives that I remembered, I was starving in a basement. My parents decided it was best if they ate the food available instead of giving it to me."It was better this way," they told me. *Was this my food issue? Did I always feel like I could never fill myself up? I hated to go long hours without food. Was my soul programmed from this past life?* When I 'died' in that lifetime, the hypnotist asked me what I saw or felt. I explained that my Grandmother (my father's mother) was there to wrap me in a big hug. I was enveloped in pure love. This was exactly what had happened to me during the meditation in my Reiki training. My Grandmother told me, "This time wasn't about you dear. It was about your parents." *Could this also be a message that my relationship with my parents in this lifetime was about them and not me? Would I have a parallel life soul lesson? How does one believe in such 'nonsense'? Seeing mediums and doing past life regressions was so different than worshipping in church. I seemed to actually connect with something more.*

Shamus and I at the Patriot's game.

A year after going to the baseball game with my younger son, I had the opportunity to go see a Patriot's game with my older son and his fiancée at the time. The Patriot's were playing the Tennessee Titans. Our family was always involved in baseball, with both boys playing since t-ball. We loved to attend Red Sox games. As a family, we never really watched much football. At the football game, I asked my son how he got interested in football. He explained that it was the trip to Tennessee when him and his Dad went to visit my husband's brother, Tyler's father. His Uncle John took him to see a Tennessee Titan's game. We thought it was interesting that the Patriot's were playing against the Titans while we were at Gillette Stadium. While we were talking, he said maybe Grandpa was here. I said maybe even Tyler. *I cherish these types of conversations with my kids and am so glad that they are open to understanding our connection to Heaven.* Later on that week, we found out that Tyler's father was also at the same game!

After my father passed away, we sold all three properties for the estate. One of the first properties to go was the family camp on Lake Elmore. I hadn't told my Father when he was alive that most likely it would be too much for me to be able to afford to keep the camp. It needed a lot of work and it would be difficult with multiple people owning a property. This bothered me a lot and I felt sick inside. For

My family's camp when my Great Grandmother purchased it in the 1940's.

weeks, I prayed to my father for forgiveness. He, like Mom had, came to me in a dream. It was so real. He was sitting with me on a couch. He was younger, like my mom was in the other dream I had months prior. He handed me a photo album, opened up to the page where there was a picture of him cooking bacon and eggs on an open fire at camp. He cooked Sunday morning breakfasts for about 75 people when I was a little girl. I immediately wake up from the dream and think, *What was my father's message? A voice from within says,* **"You will always have the memories."** *I think of my trips with Patrick and Shamus. Making memories helps us feel close to our loved ones. This was what life was really about. It wasn't about things, it was about people.* I begin to tell people about my dream. *I believe my father forgave me for selling the camp. I felt he understood.*

I recently drove by my father's camp. The new owners had torn the camp down the year before, leaving only the foundation in the ground. They had built a beautiful new house on top of the old foundation. The foundation was built when I was a kid about 10 years old. We dug it out by hand. With help from another family, we had taken each load of dirt out of the cellar by wheelbarrow.

They tore down everything my father had built. They only left the foundation. I felt horrible yet again. *Had my father really forgiven me for selling the camp? He was always so proud of the camp he had rebuilt over the years. Seeing the camp gone made it real. There were now new people living there making new memories.*

My father's camp before they tore it down.

I drove by this new house where my family camp used to be but it was not a camp any longer. This place looked like people could live there year round. It was beautiful- gray vinyl siding with pretty white trim. I decide to stop by to see a relative who lives at the other end of the lake. When visiting, Marion says, "Oh- did you see your father's camp? Isn't it beautiful? I think your father would be smiling and so happy that they used that foundation and made that camp, well really a new house, look so nice!" *I was floored. Wait, what? She was thinking in the positive, not the negative. Wow, I think, imagine having her for a mom growing up! Would I ever be able to reverse my internal programming to think in the positive? I knew I had to in order to be healed. Be easy on yourself, I think. It will happen but you will need to work at it! All of my horrible feelings wondering about my father's forgiveness disappear. They are replaced with him smiling at me.*

"The simple things are also the most extraordinary things, and only the wise can see them." ~Paull Coelho

I was so good at giving others advice about chasing dreams and finding their true calling. I would try to inspire them but I realized that I wasn't making the changes in my life. I knew that I needed to take a risk and follow my dreams. My true calling was coming in unexpected surprises. The dimes were leading me in a different direction.

"This is what we call love. When you are loved, you can do anything in creation. When you are loved, there's no need at all to understand what's happening, because everything happens within you." ~ Paul Coelho

Chapter 17 THE Dime

"I'd finally come to understand what it had been: a yearning for a way out, when actually what I had wanted to find was a way in."
~Cheryl Strayed

Looking back, I am thankful that I was introduced to God and attended church as a child. For me, it will always be a part of who I am. There was never any question for me and I never doubted the fact that there is some sort of God or Spirit that is more than the physical human life we all experience. *What I doubted the most were signs from Heaven, including the inner-most voice inside me. I wasn't sure if the messages were real or if I was imagining them.*

"Like a wink from your grandfather, these winks are communicating God's message to you: 'Hey kid, I'm thinking about you-right now." ~SQuire Rushnell

When I turned 20 I remember a conversation I had with God. I told him that he wouldn't "see me" for awhile in my twenties. I explained that I wouldn't be attending church for awhile but, "most likely" I would be back in my thirties. Why I conscientiously thought this, I have no idea. When my father wasn't able to attend church, he would always say, "pray for me". I thought the same thing and hoped that someone would pray for me. I guess every 20 year old thinks they know everything and it is part of the breaking away that everyone needs to go through. For me, the game of life gave me some challenges before I hit the thirty mark. I had back surgery when I turned 27, then went into a deep depression and realized that I was trying to numb both my physical and emotional pain with alcohol. There was no where else to turn but to God. I did attend AA meetings at first to get sober, but in a place where I thought there were "automatic" friends, I felt out of place yet again. I was able to get enough tools in my toolkit to be able to get sober and free, but I never felt accepted by the people there. I had to take care of myself and my family first and foremost so I instead went to counseling for years. I was slowly digging myself out of the hole I had dug. I was learning to play the game in the ballpark with some tough at bats but I had God by my side. I was learning to take a different path instead of trying to go through the rock. I feel that now I am at another turning point in my life. *Was I going to take the path all shiny and new or the path which had been stomped on by shoes? Would I be able to make the changes I needed to make?*

I spend so much time in my head thinking about how I feel or how other people feel. I can sense how someone feels before they even speak to me. I know if someone is scared, mad, or happy. For me, emotions affect everything I do. I reflect on different things I have learned along the way and the idea that I am an empath. "Think like your life depended on it." Emotions, including faith, are the one thing that Science can't take into consideration when looking at the results of some medical or educational experiments. For instance, medical science will conduct an experiment to show the results of some new promising drug for heart disease. They can track everything except the emotions of the person. The drug might work on some people, but it might also be about their thoughts. *Have they ever asked the person if they believe in God? Would this have an affect on the experiment?* Emotions are the one variable that you can't control in an experiment. The same thing is happening in education. The government wants "research based" programs to be used in schools. The research doesn't take into account that we are spiritual beings having a human experience. The spiritual part is what controls our emotions. No one program will ever work for everyone because we are all unique human beings, caught up in our own thoughts and emotions. *Did I think like this because I was an empath? Could I really feel others' emotions? Hadn't I guessed some of my students' thoughts when they were nervous or scared? How would we be able to design a research project about sensing the things we cannot see?*

"**Eventually I learned to sense these fields, intuitively, without having to use my hands at all. To a psychic, a person's energy field is as real as the scent of her perfume, her smile, or the warm red color of her hair. This work had validated what I felt for a long time. There was more to human beings than their physical qualities, a palpable essence extended outward. Before I had no way to confirm what I sensed to be true. But, now another missing piece of the puzzle was falling into place.**"~ Dr. Judith Orloffe

Judith uses the words "psychic" and I think back to what my mother told me about "those" types of people. They are kind of, you know, crazy. *But what if I was one? What if I was one of the crazies my mother talked about all the time? Did being an empath make me a "psychic" and, if it did, what exactly did **that** mean? I most definitely was able to feel people's energy as Judith describes. Maybe I was taking on my mother's feelings. Was I just like her? Was I always worried what others might think of me? Was I worried about "keeping up my appearances"? What did I need to do differently? How would I take responsibility for myself instead of blaming her? Had I been so focused on her that I forgot to admit who I am? I struggled with being a public school teacher who also believed in God. My anxiety was my insecurity about myself and who I was. Especially admitting that I am an empath. Time to get honest with myself.*

Two years after my father's death, my younger son was continuing his search for a home to purchase. Most of the houses in the area were either too high priced or needed too much work. I was finishing my Master's work, finishing up my 27th year teaching and beginning a new job as Curriculum Director. I had a two week vacation before I would start working full time. In my new role, I would have to work all summer; something that was new to me after so many years of having the summer off. I was in the middle of an intense online law class for administrators, but knew that this two week window would be the only time I could help my son look for a home to purchase. We scheduled some showings with a friend of mine, Brenda- a Realtor whom I had worked for previously. We schedule three showings on Friday night, the first two houses are not even ones that I would want him to buy. When we go to the third house, it was perfect for him. The house itself was a mess, but we could see past that. *Of course, my fears appear. Is this too much for him? Is the land too wet? I sense my son's stress and wonder if this is what we should be doing. I reassure him that we are here to help him but I think this is a good fit for him.*

The contracts are drawn up and negotiations begin. Over the course of the next two months, we would go back and forth about details of the house, including the septic system, the deck railings and other such things. At times, we weren't sure if the deal would go through. Eventually, the closing was scheduled for August 31st. This would be about two years after my father's death and it happened to be the first day of school in my new district. This would be the first year that nobody would miss me on the first day of school!

On the morning of the closing, I stop by one of the schools during their opening day activities. Excitement in the air, marking a brand new school year. Goodbye to the summer days; hello to learning. I leave the school and begin the commute to my new office. As I fly out of town, around the corner, I realize that I am going a little too fast for this particular sharp corner. I'm in my head thinking of not being in a classroom this year. I'm also nervous about the closing today. I'm driving but I'm on automatic pilot, just like when I was driving to my father's camp the day his heart was breaking. The car behind me thinks that I am going too fast too. I realize it is a sheriff's car when I see his blue lights. I pull over. I was in my head driving; in another world. I fumble with my words, "I have no idea why you pulled me over.....Oh, I was speeding?"

I had no idea what the speed limits were on my new commute. He was about to let me in on that secret. "Do you have something on your mind?" he asks. I nervously spit out- "I have a new job, it's the first day of school and my son is closing on his house today. My car is loaded and I have a lot to do." I know that a closing can have things go wrong, even at the last minute. As a realtor, it was always a concern that an attorney would find some legal problem and the deal wouldn't go through. I can't find my registration as he asks me if I have even been pulled over. "No," I respond, "except for once when I had a light out." He gave me a nice reminder to slow down because he would hate to have something happen to me or anyone else; explaining that even a small car like mine can do a lot of damage.

A warning, in more ways than one. A warning about the speed limit, but also a warning for me to get out of my head and back in the present moment. This is always a challenge for me. I'm either in the past or the future, and rarely enjoying the moment. I needed to learn to enjoy the cup of tea, as Brian Weiss suggests. It's also a warning that life is short and I need to think about how I am living my life. *What daily choices are you making that will make your life the best life possible? Use that golden ticket.*

I have difficulty finding time to exercise. Well, I guess I have the time but I prioritize and don't put exercise first. I remember one time asking a student, whose father was a doctor, how his father had the time to run everyday. I knew that a doctor most likely would have long hours and would most definitely be tired when he got home. I did not expect this response. He said, "You find time to eat, don't you? Well, your body needs exercise and food so why not find time for both?" Although I had all of the tools about exercise, eating healthy, meditating, praying and so on, I hadn't been taking the time during the day to practice them on a regular basis. Until I do, I most likely won't see a change in my life. *How will I be able to do this? What will it take to "motivate me"? A voice whispers, "take your time. Start small." How will being in the moment help me heal? Will it help me enjoy life more?*

"I don't live in either my past or my future. I'm interested only in the present. If you can concentrate always on the present, you'll be a happy man. Life will be a party for you, a grand festival, because life is the moment we're living now." ~ Paul Coelho

During the walk through the house the evening prior to my son's closing, the place was a disaster. It was still being lived in (most of the time during a walk through, houses are empty) and it was filthy dirty. *What if they didn't clean it out in time for the closing tomorrow?* I was so worried about whether or not this was a good choice for my son. He, on the other hand, took a walk outside to the apple trees on the front lawn, picks up and bites into an apple. As he approaches, he says, "Everything looks good to me!" I know he is dreaming of the deer who might be eating those same apples later in the fall. Brenda laughs and tells me that she knows we are going to find a dime here somewhere. *Maybe, I think.*

The closing goes smoothly and we begin moving him in right after. The house is very dirty so I begin scrubbing down the kitchen. The reality that both of my children are now homeowners hits me as I clean. They worked hard and were living close by each other. I work on setting up the kitchen. After hours of scrubbing, I go to vacuum the bedroom, making sure the carpet is clean before they come back with the bed. The previous owners had a large breed dog and a cat. Pet hair is everywhere. I am vacuuming every edge and corner where the hair has been accumulating for years. I am inside the closet, on my hands and knees vacuuming when a dime is caught where the closet door is attached to the floor. With the light from the window shining in on the dime, I take a photo to post on Facebook. Brenda, our Realtor and friend, comments on my post, "I KNEW IT!" Soon after, I find a penny. This, I feel, was my Mom. Everyone would be focused on the dime. Some of my friends on Facebook had heard about the dime on the mountain and here was another dime!

"He has made beautiful everything in his time. He has also set eternity the human heart; yet no one can fathom what God has done from beginning to end. " Ecclesisastes 3:11

Was this really another dime from my dad? To go with the rest of my collection? Did he need God's help arranging for me to find the dime? Was he sending a message to my son that he was here with him?

It's now the last day of our vacation in Florida. I stop writing to run on the beach. Grounding me and making sure that I don't float away; so caught up in my writing. I needed to take a break. I try to breathe in the smell of the ocean and absorb the sunshine. I search furiously on the ground for a dime. He must be here. I see many seashells about the same size as a dime, but no dimes. I'm afraid that I won't remember every single message that is coming to me now. I envision the caretaker pointing to his head, saying, "I'm trying to remember them in my brain." I worry that if I do decide to make this into a book, the signs won't be seen as fitting into the dime story. I think they do. The dime story is so much more than the dimes sent from Heaven.

My husband arrives and, noticing I am almost out of pages in my journal, asks if I am almost done. I shake my head no. Then he says, "Well, I guess you'll know when you are done." The waves roll in, the seagulls squawk and people continue up and down the beach.

"So we fix our eyes not on what is seen, but on what is unseen. For what is seen is temporary, but what is unseen is eternal." ~2Corinthians 4:18

I think back to the conversation with a stranger on the beach. I had shared with him that I was stepping out of my comfort zone to write a book. He will be a part of the book. He shares with me that he was saying a prayer on his walk and decided to stop and talk to me. He tells me he is no minister, just a man living the life Jesus speaks of in the gospel of John. He says, "I'm not sure what religion you believe in, but my guiding religion is the Roman Catholic Church." I laugh and share that I converted to be a Catholic because my husband's family was Catholic. I tell him that my father told me that, "We are all talking to the same guy." We finish up chatting and he blesses me. Even though he wasn't a minister, he reminds me of the time on the mountain when my father "phoned" me. No, the dime story is not finished. The dimes will never be done as this story will be passed on and on. When people find a dime, they will know that someone from Heaven is with them.

"Allow me to change your doubts into questions." ~William Sloane Coffin

Writing the dime story was a process to accepting myself. It will help me heal. I continue to feel the need to write my story; asking for answers. Answers are given; whenever I listen and when the timing is decided by the universe to be perfect. Messages from angels can be almost anything. *While in the pool, a woman says, "Hey Ty!" in the same southern drawl that sounds like my sister-in-law calling to her son Tyler. But, Tyler isn't really here, or is he? I check the time.* **5:55.** *Oh yeah- that is when angels are around my son, Patrick.*

"Each of us has a destiny, and there is absolutely no excuse not to fulfill it. We cannot use our weakness as an excuse because God says that His strength is made perfect in weakness." 2 Corinthians 12:9

"We cannot use the past as an excuse because God tells us through the apostle Paul that if any person is in Christ, he is a new creature; old things have passed away, and all things have become new." ~2 Corinthians 5:17

Could this really be true? Would God's strength help me continue to write this book, be healed and learn to live life a different way? Was I going to lead in a different way than what I imagined when I had received my Master's degree in education to become an administrator?

"Yes," my angels respond.

"Stop your inner critic dead in her tracks and tell the lies to get lost because you are enough." ~Robert Jones

I work so hard the first day cleaning my son's new home that I am physically exhausted. We leave our son alone the next day to settle in and enjoy his new home without Mom and Dad around. The next day, my husband and I go to help him with a few things around the house.

My son and husband go to the roof to work on the chimney and I begin to clean the nasty carpet in the spare bedroom. I know my son didn't really understand how dirty it really was.

As I clean, I continue to worry. *Was buying this house too much for my son? Did I guide him in the right direction? Will he be able to afford it? Would my father have approved of the purchase of the house? Would my father have liked it here?*

God Grant me the Serenity
To accept the things I cannot change
Courage to change the things I can
And the wisdom to know the difference.
~Reinhold Niebuhr (1892-1971)

We had made the decision to purchase the house and we were blessed with resources to help him if he needed more support. He would be ok. This was the perfect spot for him. *The positive voice inside me trying to convince me. If only I would listen...instead of feeling anxiety and worry within my entire body.*

Again, making sure to get every edge of the carpet, I am almost finished vacuuming when I notice I didn't really get around the spot where the cable cords come up through the wood flooring. I go back to the spot and notice a coin. I think it is a nickel. It is tucked down in the hole in the floor, next to the cords. I pull away the vacuum; afraid that I might vacuum it up. *I'm not sure I can get it. It is really jammed down in there. A nickel, my mind thinks. Not really too important if I can't get it.* **I could just leave it there.**

Finally, it comes out and I hold it up to look at it. This is not a nickel. This is a dime, but not like the dime I found the other day in the closet. This dime is a very **particular** dime.

This dime is the **same dime that was in my father's collection. A Liberty Head dime.** Instead of having Franklin D. Roosevelt's profile, this type of dime has the Liberty wearing a winged cap, symbolizing **"freedom of thoughts."**

This is the very exact type of dime that my father had made into necklaces for all of his family. The year on the dime was 1936, one year later than my father's birth year. I run out to my son and husband who are on the roof. I holler up to them, **"I found a LIBERTY HEAD DIME! You know- the kind that was in my dad's collection. It's exactly like the one in our necklaces. You cannot call me crazy anymore!! This is proof- for sure!"** They look down at me from on top of the roof. *They have to believe now, I think. My Father gave me the biggest 'God Wink' if I ever did see one!*

I think, just as Neale Donald Walsch does in his story about his NDE when he said,

"Am I being played here? Is somebody kidding me?" Then the other voice inside him speaks, 'That is not necessary. Your truth will never be forgotten. It can be neither proven or disproven. It simply is.....Nothing matters.'"

I wonder, does it matter if anyone believes my story? Does it matter if I share it? Will people believe that my father was using the 'Spirit Connection System' I had explained to him? Had he placed a physical object yet again for me to discover?

Was my father helping God give me the signs I needed at the right time? Was my Dad helping God control "the knobs" he wondered about when he was here on earth? Did all of my angels in Heaven who I envisioned as cheerleaders help show signs to me? Did everyone have people in Heaven helping us navigate life's journey? Showing everyone, or at least those who want to believe, that there is something bigger than us?

"We are not thinking machines that feel, rather we are feeling machines that think." ~Antonio Damasio

My son and husband look down at me as I scream at them. *What should I do with this dime?* I take a picture and post a picture of the dime on Facebook. One of the first comments was, *"Seriously?"* Yeah, I think. **Seriously. This is serious. This is a sign like no other sign.** *Nobody can argue this sign, I think. Nobody understands the conversations I* *had with my father. This story is so much more than dimes. It is a story like no other.*

My son was the best man for his older brother's wedding this year. His speech made me laugh and cry. The one paragraph that meant the most to me was the following:

"This summer my brother and I were riding around some back roads, talking about our lives, and he said something I will always remember. He said, 'Just be yourself. Don't ever try to be anything but yourself.' Shamus has lived his entire life by those words. For anybody who knows him well, they know he is a goofy, good hearted, out going guy. And I respect him for that, because he is always himself." ~Patrick Morrissey 8/18/18

I am ready to take my sons' advice. I mean, I am who I am, right?

Epilogue More Than a Dime

"It's all fine and good to imagine what life would be like somewhere else. It takes some courage to leave and go somewhere new. To head out to the great unknown. But what happens if upon taking the first step, something goes wrong? Maybe it was a bad idea to leave in the first place? Maybe it's best to turn back and stay put? After all, the devil you know is better than the devil you don't. Or, maybe if you have the right people with you, they will give you the courage to keep going." ~Simon Sinek

One might ask~ Is this the end of the dime story? The title of the dime story is More Than a Dime because the story is about so much more than the dime. For me, the dime was the key to me believing everything that I had learned and experienced over the years. It was also a sign to keep learning more about myself. When I shared my dime story with people, they were always touched, most of the time people got goosebumps. *What was this all about? When I began to write, I realized that this story is so much more than dimes.*

The people who I shared my dime story with encouraged me to keep writing and are my tribe. They are the ones who love me just as I am. They help me believe in myself and know that the risk is worth it. Once I decided that my story was "More Than a Dime", I couldn't turn back no matter how much anxiety or fear I had. I knew that it would be worth it.

I listened to **Jason Gray's song "I Will Rise Again"**. It helped give me the courage to continue writing.

Just like new life in the spring starts again after a cold winter, I was ready to start a fresh new season of life. I will rise again each day, navigating life, wherever it brings me. *Thy Will be done.*

Dad's funeral
Here is what I read at my Father's funeral:
August 29, 2015

Jim Palmer to most of you. Dad to us four kids. Grandpa to all of his grandchildren. There are so many things to talk about when I think of our Dad. His kindness, his sense of giving to others, his love for our Mother, his love for his kids and his grand-kids, his love of his church family, his faith in doing the right thing, his hard work, his sense of pride, his humor, his knowledge of how things work, his curiosity, his interest in getting to know other people, the way his face would light up when visitors came.

I was able to get to know my Dad over the last few months more than I ever knew him in my entire life. I always knew our Dad was special, but I really learned it this year. We all got to hear the story about when he asked Mom to marry him, it was going to either be her or the Volkswagon car. He couldn't afford both, but would take her if she was interested. Well, luckily she was interested!

I can't really explain my Dad's sense of humor. He would tell a story and it would be so funny. Then, I would try to retell it and it just didn't work. I think it had some-thing to do with the twinkle in his eye and the smirk on his face. It was also the way he worded it, it always came out so that we would all laugh. Even though he missed Mom every day, he learned to enjoy having all of us around. We got to hear stories we had never heard before. I think my two sons will always remember the "boy scout juice"- as he told them how to light a fire in the furnace. He said, And then it goes "boom". Well, probably they don't want you doing that these days. Or how about hide the thimble with the Grandkids. They were looking and looking and Grandpa says, "I ate it!"

Dad learned early on he probably shouldn't speak in inappropriate language. One time while working on a car, he was not speaking in very good language, he came around the corner to find the minister there. Another time, while playing over a bank near his house, his Mother came out and said, "You know I can hear very clearly everything you are saying." Whoops!...

Dad loved each and every one of his kids and Grandkids. Each of you held a special place in his heart. Even though his heart attack kept him from working at the garage, it was actually sort of a blessing. It meant that he was home and ready to babysit any Grandkid that needed a place to be. He was ready to pick up kids after school at any-time. He was ready to go play outside with them. ....I get asked a lot what my two sons are doing. When I tell them that Shamus is an Auto-Tech, I also say that I might have been a carrier of the Auto gene, but I never was able to use it in my life. It went straight to Shamus. When I think of Patrick, he is very similar to Dad when he is curious as to how things work. Dad was always about problem solving....

To us he was Dad, but to many of you, he was Jim Palmer, owner of the business Palmer's Inc. He loved all of his customers over the years, his many employees and enjoyed getting to know business associates from all over...There are so many memo-ries from Palmer's Inc. that it is difficult to put into words. We all grew up playing in the tires, watching Dad work his magic on cars, and helping whenever we could. Pumping gas was always a part of our teenage years and this is where we all began to meet the many customers who loved to go to Palmers.

I cannot express our thanks enough to Merrilee Perrine and all of the caregivers from Love Is. They all made this past year the best that it could be. He enjoyed getting to know each and every one of his caregivers. You all helped him through the difficulty of losing his wife. He had a whole new set of friends that he could share his life with. He always felt so proud to introduce his new friends to people stopping by to visit. I know his favorite was Merrilee- oh how he picked on her! He was so excited when she started to cook for him. Well, one day she made some cookies and when she brought them out, he was surprised by the size of the cookie. He said, "Well, now THAT is a cookie. I guess I won't need two or three. One will be just fine." If only you could have seen the expression in his eyes to go along with his words- that is what made us love him. A big thank you to everyone who helped this past year to make it so Dad could stay home. It was definitely a team effort with all of us kids, grandkids, cousins, relatives, friends, home health, Love Is and the doctors who still made house calls. Marisa and Alden visiting every week to help him was so appreciated. This helped him so much. Uncle David and Aunt Jean visiting for coffee every week. These visits helped him feel closer to Mom. With everyone working together, Dad had a great 8 months. People always told Dad how lucky he was to have everyone here to help him. I'm sure all the caregivers, friends and family can agree that we were the lucky ones.

Dad's church family was so important to him. His Mother was the person who taught him about Faith and then it trickled down to all of us. Church was always a big part of all of our lives and it sure has helped us get through the rough spots. We thank him for teaching us about his faith and we thank all of the people in the church whom he cared so much for...The joy on his face that day was priceless, talking with his church family. He especially enjoyed Ray's weekly visits. He could always count on Ray coming by to visit him. He loved that Ray felt like family.

This past year Dad learned a lot about technology. He was a regular check in on Facebook, learned the fastest way to get anything you wanted was through Amazon Prime, Facetimed with Monica on the beach in Florida, Facetimed with Melissa and Ray at their wedding, watched UVM basketball games on his iPad. Now his connection with us is through all kinds of signs. The Spirit Communication system is working for him now. We all know he is around us.

It was great to have Dad at camp this summer. We all learned to take the time to be with you because we didn't know how long you would be with us. Our hearts are now empty but it is filled with great memories... Camp has always had so many memories that we will keep with us. Deb learning to ski with one ski before you- sorry but you were dropping the wrong ski. Me- first time on one ski and I tried to splash Brian but ended up crashing into the dock. The many hours all of us begged to go skiing. The Sunday breakfast. Nothing better than a 100 or so people and scrambled eggs and bacon over an open fire. Elmore will forever be a part of all of us and all of the many families we were connected with. There are just too many families to mention here but so many people have shared their memories of good times with our family. You all know who you are. We are all thinking of you when we remember our Mom and Dad and how much they loved all of you. Especially Eldon, who now has lost his best friend, who was more like a brother. We are thinking of you today.

While taking care of my Dad, we all experienced his way of thinking. His biggest question was always, "How is this going to work?" This question was used all the time, when he was trying to figure out how his care was going to happen to getting showers from the Home Health nurses, to how he was going to live at camp full time. His mind thought like a mechanic his entire life. It was the way he was wired. He thought maybe another surgery on his heart might keep that engine going just like an oil change or a new transmission on a car. If they could just keep working on it, it would run forever. That is the goal of every mechanic. Keep that car running. I know your car is still running, just this time you are in spirit form and now your engine will run forever. Thanks for being there for me at the top of the mountain yesterday.

Part 2 Who am I and why am I like this?

"Life is not primarily a quest for pleasure, as Freud believed, or a quest for power, as Alfred Adler taught, but a quest for meaning. The greatest task for any person is to find meaning in his or her life." ~Victor E. Frankl

Most of the dime story was written while on vacation in Indian Shores, Florida. My husband and I vacation there in April to get away from the long winters in Vermont. This year I was in a lot of pain and the doctors couldn't figure out what was causing my pain. I hadn't slept for longer than 1 to 2 hours at a time for many months. I decided that I needed to try to figure out how to solve my medical problems. I understood that emotions cause physical problems in our bodies from years of reading books like Louise Hay's, You Can Heal Your Life and The secret language of your body: The essential guide to health & wellness. Normally when I go on vacation, I read books. This time, I would begin to write my "dime story". During the process of writing the dime story, I realized that it was so much more than a dime. The dimes were a powerful message to me from Heaven. Heaven was trying to get my attention so that I would have a deeper understanding. Through writing this book and consulting with five different doctors, I am finally on the road to recovery. My pain could not be healed with medicine alone.

I had to do the emotional work and alternative healing too. *I had to learn to accept and love myself, especially the fact that I am an empath. Discovering I am an empath, changed my perspective and my writing.*

I never understood writing and how it might help me. I didn't understand people who said things like, "the words seem to come from somewhere else." When I started to write, I experienced this for the first time in my life. When I let go of the beliefs instilled in me since childhood, I was able to connect with my soul. When I did this, it opened up a whole new world for me. It was like the universe heard my thoughts and knew I was ready.

While writing, my crown chakra was so open I had to work at grounding myself. There are seven energy systems in our bodies, starting with the base of our spine to the top of our head. They are all associated with different colors and meanings. Here is a list: 1. Root chakra (red), base of spine 2. Sacral chakra (orange), just above the base of your spine 3. Solar plexis(yellow), the stomach area 4. Heart chakra(green), over the heart 5. Throat chakra (blue), throat area 6. Third eye chakra (dark purple), a little above the eyes, in the middle of your forehead 7. Crown chakra (light purple). My favorite color is purple and it is because when my crown chakra is open I feel connected to my intuition and the spirit world. When I am in this place, I feel absolutely wonderful and pain free, but I have to ground myself. Grounding is about connecting me back to earth. The best ways to ground myself are meditation, swimming or being in nature.

"As you journey to your destiny, you will occasionally find yourself at a crossroads in your career- a new path will suddenly appear, taking you into a whole new direction...Regardless of the circumstances, one thing is certain- you will feel uncertain." ~ SQuire Rushnell

Turning 50 affected me in a way I was not really prepared for. It wasn't a typical "mid-life" crisis. I didn't want to go buy a convertible. It was a reflection of where I have been so far in this life and what I want to do next. As I was reflecting on my life, I thought of my own children. My husband and I now have the "empty nest". I enjoy the freedom and have more time on my hands. My children don't need me as much. I had no plans whatsoever to become a writer. It wasn't even on my radar. I thought writing was for "other people". Once I decided to turn this story into a book, I knew I was on the right path..

"In fact, I believe an awareness of our diminished time on this planet offers the advantage of urgency." ~Joni B. Cole

Had I taught my own kids enough about life? Had I shared with them my stories and my beliefs? Had I let them make their own choices in life to learn their lessons?- which surely would be different than my lessons. What had I learned from them? What would they do when I was gone? Would they make some of the same mistakes I had made? Would me sharing what I had learned about life help them navigate their lives better? What was I going to do with all of the free time I had? I had always worked and enjoyed being a Mom. I didn't like to sit around and do nothing. I wasn't that type of person!

Losing both of my parents within eight months of each other, I realized I had raised my own children very differently than the way I was raised. I had tried to give them the support they needed to navigate life in a different way. I had taught them about God, faith and gratitude. I showed them that I not only cared about them, but I loved them unconditionally, very similar to how God loves them. No matter what happened or the choices they made, I would always love them. I might not always like the decisions they made, but that would never change my love for them. I taught them to love others and be kind. *It was important to me!*

I am an empath or a highly sensitive person (HSP)- whatever you want to call it. All my life I had just wanted to be "normal". Knowing and understanding what it means to be an empath helped me learn to accept myself. This meant accepting that I needed to take care of myself and that this did not define me. In education we talk about students who have Autism, but we don't say Autistic students. Autism does not define who they are. The same is true for an empath. I am a person who is an empath, not an empathic person. This has two very different meanings. An empathic person can feel what the other person is feeling because they have felt the same thing in their life. For instance, someone who has lost both of their parents can understand and feel empathy for me because I lost both of my parents. An empath is a person with an intuitive ability to know the mental or emotional state of another individual. Some dictionaries mention it to be "paranormal" ability instead of intuitive ability. *My worst fear coming true- being different and not normal!* I choose to define it as an intuitive knowing, rather than something weird out of a Sci-fi movie.

When I started reading about empaths and highly sensitive people, I remember thinking, "Oh my! There are other people in the world who are like me!" My nervous system is built differently and I have the ability to take on other people's emotions. After learning about empaths, I didn't feel like such a freak anymore. There are other parts of my life that are affected. I have food sensitivities, sleep, addiction, and anxiety issues to share a few. Awareness and knowledge is important. I wasn't aware that I was an empath so I was confused most of my life. I hope by sharing my story it will bring awareness to our world, especially in education. I want people to understand what it is like to be an empath. Teachers and parents need to understand that a child's emotions are critical to the learning process. It is difficult to learn if a child doesn't feel like he or she belongs.

This next section of the book is about my healing journey. Writing my dime story helped me become aware that I was an empath. *What did this mean? Did being an empath affect my entire life story? How would I need to change my life in order to stay healthy? By doing so, would I then be able to accept myself and heal my heart so that I would be able to avoid heart disease? How can I learn to change my internal dialogue?* Chapter by chapter, I will share how coins and coincidences help me find healing and peace.

Chapter 1 My Young Self

"We are programmed to attend to, store, and recall negative information over positive information, so much so that, according to one famous finding in the realm of relationship psychology, it takes at least five positive interactions to make up for just one negative one." ~Joni B. Cole

When I originally wrote chapter one of this book, it didn't look like the chapter you read. I spent a lot of time blaming and being angry at my mother. It was easier for me to remember the negative than the positive parts of my childhood. I don't want to seem ungrateful for my childhood because I know there were a lot of things I was grateful for. When I went to rewrite the first chapter, I had a lot of knowledge about what being an empath meant for me. I realized that the reason I didn't fit in to my family was because I was extremely sensitive and an empath. This made childhood more challenging for me, even when to others it seemed like I had a great family. By looking from the inside, instead of focusing on the outside, I was able to see how accepting myself was one the most important parts of my soul's journey.

In 1996 I had back surgery to remove a herniated disc at my SI/L5 joint, at the base of my spine. Although the pain I was having while writing this book was different, it was in the same general area. I was having bladder issues and was beginning to go through menopause. Not exactly something I am excited about sharing in a book with the world- but here I am! Louise Hay says that emotions cause us "dis-ease." If you look up the emotional message that is connected to sciatica pain, you will find things like, "...weren't able to express our true feelings or fears, we don't feel safe or secure." (retrieved from https://ravenstarshealingroom.wordpress.com/2017/03/26/the-metaphysics-of-sciatic-and-peripheral-pain/) It goes on to say that because of this, a person might become shy or reclusive. That was me! As a child, I was scared to share my feelings and became the quiet kid. I was lost among the crowds and wasn't sure of myself.

As an empath, I physically absorb emotions of the people around me. Imagine I am sitting outside in the sunshine. I can feel the warmth of the sunshine in my entire body. Now, imagine that sunshine being another person's energy. The person is sitting next to me and I absorb their positive feelings and it feels just as good as the sunshine on my face. This was like the Up with People concert! I actually feel good inside because the person near me is happy and is showing me love. I feel it physically and emotionally, just like the sun makes my body feel warm inside. Now, change the scene to sitting outside in the snow. It's cold and my body temperature starts to go down. I want to get warm, but I can't. This is what it feels like to sit next to a person who has negative energy. I feel it on the inside of my body, physically, as if the emotions were my own. Without the necessary skills needed to understand and separate from those feelings, the person's energy affects me just like they were my own feelings.

I have difficulty with my own feelings because of how I was raised. We didn't talk about feelings and I stuffed them all inside. But now enter all the feelings of all of the people around me every day. I can't always distinguish between what are my feelings or the person's emotions next to me. And all of these feelings get stuck inside my body and can make my body ill. This is what it is like to be an empath. I never knew this about myself and I never had the words to understand what was happening. Brene Brown says that the emotion that is most contagious is anxiety. I was "catching" that a lot these days. Once I was aware, I would start to distinguish what were my emotions and what emotions belonged to others. I am slowly learning how to stop absorbing feelings and emotions from everyone else. I separate myself and try not to let any negative energy from others inside my body. Of course, the people with sunshine always feel great but I had to learn to leave the ice cubes alone!

"We actually feel others' emotions, energy, and physical symptoms in our own bodies, without the usual defenses that most people have" ~Dr. Judith Orloff

I'll give you an example that happened to me recently. I was at a meeting with about fifteen people. The presenters were sharing their work and then asked us to turn and talk to our neighbor. During the presentation, I seriously wanted to fall asleep. It wasn't because I was bored or hungry or hadn't slept well the night before. I had no idea what was happening. I thought I might have to get up and take a walk just to stay awake. The presenters asked us to turn and talk to the person next to us. I turned to the person next to me and we began chatting. She was pretty upset about the presentation and thought it was a waste of everyone's time. I immediately recognized that my "sleepiness" was me absorbing her negative energy. I quickly used one of my new strategies to block the negative energy and then I was wide awake!

I can't watch scary movies, which includes the news. If I'm not careful, I will absorb all the negativity from the TV, newspaper or radio. Today's media is so divided, especially on governmental issues, and I don't know what is the truth anymore. I simply cannot partake in the conversations. Being a Libra, I want balance and in today's media there seems to be no common ground. It physically makes me ill. While healing and writing, I shut my TV off more and more. I discovered I was much happier this way. If we think about how life used to be about one hundred years ago(or more!), our human systems were not built to take in so much information, especially negative information.

I'll use another example to try to explain how an empath is affected by having a different nervous system. I watch The Big Bang Theory on CBS. There are so many times in my life where I wish I could be like Sheldon- who does not seem to care how other people feel. But that isn't how I am built. It's almost like I am the exact opposite of Sheldon when it comes to my feelings inside. I worry about how people feel all the time and I intuitively sense other people's feelings- whether I want to or not. It isn't a choice. Information about feelings come through as an energy from others. It makes it so I am in my head worrying about how they feel instead of being in the present moment. For instance, someone might say something like, "I'm not sure about this idea." I receive all sorts of feelings with the message like, "I'm actually really angry". It's like my intuition is talking to me adding information to what the person is saying. This can be a dangerous place to be in because I might be wrong if I don't check in with that person about how they are feeling. I might "read" their emotions incorrectly and then it might cause unnecessary problems. I have learned to check in with people and not take on any emotions that aren't mine.

Sheldon and I are similar in the way that our senses can get overloaded. Too many lights, smells, and sounds can most definitely overstimulate me. I hear people talk all the time about going to concerts to see different bands or singers. For me, that is a nightmare. Not only the crowds, but the noise, sounds, smells, and lights overstimulate my sensitive body. That is not my idea of fun at all. How would I rather spend my time? *On a beach or camping in the woods.* That is my idea of a great vacation! The biggest difference between the two vacations? People and nature. I don't want to be around so many people that I become exhausted. Being outside in nature always recharges me. Most likely when I was young, playing outside helped my nervous system stay regulated.

Another thing that I learned was that empaths try to protect themselves with fat. It is like the weight I gain acts as a buffer to protect my body from absorbing another person's feelings. Once I learned the strategies to protect myself, I no longer needed the weight to protect myself. If you want to learn more, check out Judith Orloff's book The Empath's Survival Guide.

Don Miquel Ruiz wrote a book called The Four Agreements. The Four Agreements are the following: "1. Be impeccable with your word. 2. Don't take anything personally. **3. Don't make assumptions** and 4. Do your best." I find it important to note these agreements here because I want to make clear that as an empath I am never one hundred percent certain that my intuitive feelings coming from others are true or not. I never assume they are without verification from the other person. Learning about the Four Agreements changed my life, especially in my job as an educator. By not taking things personally and not assuming things, my relationships with parents, students, colleagues and friends have most definitely improved. I try to understand other people's point of view without absorbing their feelings or feeling defensive.

When learning about what it is like to be an empath, I learned about what some people call "narcissists" or "energy vampires". I'm not talking about the vampires in the movies, but people who have no sense of empathy. They don't have the capability to understand what it is like to be an empath. I have met many energy suckers in my life and am thankful that I was able to learn from them. At times, I tried to help some of them but realized that I had to let them have their own journey. They are not mine to fix. If I'm not careful about the people I am around and I happen upon an "energy sucker", they can drain my energy and I am left feeling awful. I had to learn to protect myself from some of these people.

"Happiness is the choice I make today. It does not rest on my circumstances, but on my frame of mind...In cultivating the habits of happiness, I attract the people and situations that match its frequency. I smile more often, give praise more often, give thanks more often and am glad more often. For such is my choice today." ~Marianne Williamson

I think back to my young self. We didn't have Facebook and I never heard uplifting phrases like this one. The negative self talk had been overpowering my entire life, and I hadn't realized it.

Shortly after my trip to Florida, I discovered Judith Orloff Md. She was key to discovering myself as an empath or a highly sensitive person. Through reading her memoir, I found a lot of similarities in my own life. Dr. Elaine Aron was another doctor who had a lot of research and information about HSP's. According to Dr. Aron's research,

"If you find you are highly sensitive, or your child is, I'd like you to know the following: Your trait is normal. It is found in 15 to 20% of the population—too many to be a disorder, but not enough to be well understood by the majority of those around you." (retrieved from https://hsperson.com/)

Dr. Aron used much of Carl Jung's research to help her with her interest in highly sensitive people. As an educator and a parent, I notice more and more children who seem to be highly sensitive. Each generation changes and we are talking more and more about feelings and emotions. Compared to my childhood, the conversation has changed from "suck it up buttercup" to "what's happening and how can we help?" Of course, there always needs to be a balance and not swing too far in one direction. Acceptance and understanding are the two things that helped me the most.

In Chapter one, I described things like: overly sensitive, liked to be outdoors, felt different than everyone else, and sensitivity to medicine or alcohol. All of these I discovered were true for empaths. Another clue was my sleeping issues. I had to learn to accept myself as an empath and figure out the gifts and the struggles. I had to understand that most people won't understand because they aren't born this way. *"I mean I am who I am, right?" I couldn't change who I was, even if I wanted to. And, there was no possible way for my parents to understand my needs when they were raising me. I knew they understood now. I could feel it. My parents were good people. They tried the best that they could!*

"I feel it is so important not to have judgment and fear towards myself. When my inner dialogue is telling me I'm safe, unconditionally loved, and accepted, then I radiate energy outward and change my outside world accordingly. My outer life is actually only a reflection of my inner state." ~Anita Moorjani

"Intuition was a gift I had to grow into." ~Dr. Judith Orloff

I remember the first time I heard that I should embrace my gift of being an empath. This was extremely difficult for me. Every day seemed like so much work. I had to learn not to take on other people's energy. I had to learn to meditate after working all day. I had to remember to exercise and get proper nutrition. It was exhausting. *But was it worth it? I had to believe it was. It was part of my healing.*

I am so thankful for people like Judith Orloff, Anita Moorjani and John Holland who shared their struggles with accepting their intuition and gifts. As I tried to learn and accept my intuitive abilities, words like 'psychic' took on new meanings. I wasn't a crazy gypsy lady.

"The well balanced intuitive doesn't wear long white robes or carry a crystal ball. She doesn't grab your palm in the middle of the supermarket and insist on giving you a reading. Nor does she blurt out unsolicited information. She's an ordinary person; the most remarkable thing about her is that she appears un-remarkable. Her power is internalized, integrated. She doesn't have to flaunt it. As she uses her gift discerningly, radiating an understated sense of calm, we see before us someone with no need to glorify herself, someone who is profoundly simple." ~Dr. Judith Orloff

"She turned her can't into cans and her dreams into plans." ~Kobi Yamada

The more that I wrote, the more that I felt like a door to a secret vault inside me opened up. I wanted to share my story with others in the hope that what I had learned might help others. Through writing and reflecting, I was able to discover who I was and accept myself. Most people won't understand what it is like to be me. (about 80% in fact!) *Do you see any similarities in my story? Might you know an empath or a highly sensitive person? If you are an educator or a parent, do you identify with me or do your kids have similar traits? How would you help an empath?* It is especially important to nurture children who are highly sensitive or empaths. Looking back over the years, I most definitely had some students who have this gift.

"Security is mostly a superstition. It does not exist in nature...Life is either a daring adventure or nothing." ~Helen Keller

Helen's words help me share what it is like to be an empath.

How did I know I was an empath? Every single questionnaire I answered came out 100% yes. Questions like Do you have difficulty sleeping? Do you sense how others are feeling? Do you get exhausted when there are a lot of people around? Are you sensitive to loud noises? Are you sensitive to certain foods? Are you sensitive to prescription medication? Do you eat to cover up your feelings? **Every single question from every author I read, I scored 100%.** Normally in school, I always liked 100%. This time felt different. I knew that my awareness was only the first step to acceptance. If you want to look at a quick reference (without reading a whole book)- check out this website: https://ex-emplore.com/paranormal/What-is-an-Empath-Traits-signs-solutions **Remember that I can relate to every single thing on this list.**

According to some people, there are different types of Empaths. Vik Carter mentions six different types in his book EMPATH 16 Simple Habits to protect yourself, feel better and enjoy life even if you are highly sensitive. He identifies the following types of empaths: emotional, physical, intuitive, geomantic, plant and animal.

"Empaths are likely to have varying paranormal experiences throughout their lives as well, including near-death experiences (NDEs) and out-of-body experiences (OBEs)." ~Rebecca. Retrieved from https://exemplore.com/paranormal/What-is-an-Empath-Traits-signs-solutions

I shared a few of my out-of-body experiences in my dime story. (trust me- I have more!) I was always scared to talk about them with people. When I started talking about these experiences, I found a lot of other people had them too. I think back to my younger self and wish I had been able to talk with someone about these times. Hopefully, my book will begin to open up this conversation and people won't be afraid to talk about these types of experiences.

There are things I love about being an empath and things that I hate about it. I love being able to listen and follow my intuition. I know and understand we are souls having a human experience. As a teacher and a Mom, I have been able to use my intuition to help students and my own children. The challenges are learning how to care for my body out of necessity. I don't have a choice if I want to feel good. I will share some of the things that work for me, but every empath/HSP has to discover their own strategies.

About ten years ago, I learned about self regulation. I had some students in my class who needed help organizing their bodies to be ready for learning. I learned that, "A child with self -regulatory skills is able to focus his attention, control his emotions and manage his thinking, behavior and feelings." retrieved from https://day2daypar-enting.com/help-child-learn-self-regulation/ When I looked back at my childhood, I realized that I had self regulated myself by playing outside, and especially swimming all summer. Empaths love the water and I was blessed with living on the lake all summer long. As an adult I read the book, Last Child in the Woods and was forever changed. Everyone needs time in nature. There is something about the energy of the woods and earth that helps our nervous systems. We were not meant to live inside all the time and/ or spend so much time on electronics. Without exercise and nature, our bodies are not regulated to work properly. That's why hiking helps me so much. Unfortunately, I live in a climate where it isn't always nice outside and sometimes I don't go outside enough. As an educator, I find that some kids aren't outside enough and this may be why kids are struggling in school. It seems like kids today don't have a way to regulate their bodies. Because I grew up outside, I think I was able to learn better in school. As an adult I think I tried to regulate my body with food. If I was feeling tired, I might reach for coffee or a sugary treat to help me focus. Eventually, those were too much for my sensitive system. I had to learn to regulate my body in a different way.

"When you are connected to the Divine part of yourself, you are aligned with the power of pure positive energy. And that pure positive energy creates a magnetic field that draws in more pure positive energy." ~Dr. Christian Northrup

When I use the word God, I am referring to a positive life energy force coming from an all encompassing Spirit. Like the wind, we can't see it, but we can feel it. This connection with my subconscious mind is part of my regulation. By connecting with this part of me, I am better able to regulate my fight or flight mechanism of my nervous system.

I talk a lot about the two voices inside my head. One voice comes from my subconscious, a direct connection to God/Spirit and the other voice seems to come from my consciousness or ego, a direct connection to the way my brain is wired. I have heard many people say that ego stands for "edge God out". Ego is what I use to rationalize life. I take information into my brain, synthesize it and then create stories in my head based on what I have told myself to be true.

"The ego is responsible for our personal will- the part of us that must be developed enough to get up every morning and go to school and do homework or get up off the chair and exercise. Without personal will, absolutely nothing of value ever gets accomplished." ~Dr. Christian Northrup

My conscious mind is very different than my subconscious mind. Here is a perfect example of how my brain (ego) thinks differently than my soul (divine guidance).

Over the years I have experimented with Angel Cards. While writing this book, I found in one of my journals a reading from the card deck, Life Purpose Oracle Cards by Doreen Virtue.

My question was, **"Why am I here?"**

There are many ways to choose which cards are meant to answer the question I ask to the universe. I choose these cards by using a pendulum. I first spread out the cards and then hold the pendulum over each card, one at a time. When the pendulum begins swinging, I choose that card. Clockwise means yes and counterclockwise means no. If it doesn't swing, then it means no also. I usually do a past, present and future card to answer the question I asked.

Here are the answers I received. At the time they made absolutely no sense to me. Now, they have a much deeper meaning.

Past- "Creative Expression- Your soul longs to express itself creatively."

Present- "Builder- Your innate ability to build and create brings you a deep sense of accomplishment."

Future- "Spiritual Teacher- You heal with your classes, sessions and seminars."

I remember the reading and thought that I was not a creative person because I couldn't draw. This was my conscious brain talking- creating something based on past experience and knowledge. I believed ceativity was for art class and I most definitely was not an artist! *I understand now that my subconscious was speaking to me that I was creative in a very different way. I am most definitely feeling a deep sense of accomplishment as I write and have no idea how this book will change my life. I look forward to the unknown instead of trying to plan every detail. Just like the unpredictability in my job as a real estate agent, I know the universe is working to guide me in a whole new direction. I wonder what the classes, sessions and seminars will be? Because of the dimes from Heaven and this book, I have faith that Divine guidance will help my soul express itself and my brain will not get in the way. I believe that "positives outweigh the negatives."*

"When you choose thoughts that are aligned with your true nature instead of based in fear, you are always going with the most empowering options." ~Dr. Christian Northrup

An example from chapter one was my need to blame someone for what I thought was a tough childhood. That's my ego and my brain talking. My soul is more in tune with my heart and this book came from my heart. Once I looked at my childhood from my soul's perspective, I realized that I hadn't accepted myself.

Last year I watched the movie Resilience, which brought to life the research around the ACE study. ACE stands for Adverse Childhood Experiences. The research showed ten categories of experiences that affect the health of a person. In many cases the higher the score, the shorter life span for the person. Doctors were beginning to speak out about how our emotions and feelings affect our physical bodies. As an educator, I am ready to begin this discussion and how it impacts our schools. I want to bring this to light and change the educational frontier to address this need.

"When you surrender to what is and so become fully present, the past ceases to have any power. You do not need it anymore. Presence is the key. The Now is the key."~ Eckhart Tolle

Being a highly sensitive person comes with both gifts and challenges. I have to take care of my body or "machine" in different ways in order to keep my nervous system and my internal dialogue in good working order. I learned through trial and error what worked for me. I learned that being an empath helped connect me to God in a way that I always knew was possible. Through accepting myself as an empath, I began to get in touch with this part of myself. This part had been buried for a lot of years. By writing this book, I am beginning to accept myself and share my story.

Chapter 2 Meeting Jesus

If you or anyone you know is having difficulty, call the National or Local Suicide Prevention Hotline at 1-800-273-8255 and find resources at https://suicidepreventionlifeline.org/ I don't believe that suicide is the answer to anyone's problems. This was a very difficult chapter to write. I am truly amazed that I have actually lived to be as old as I am. There were many times that I thought I wanted to leave. I'm so glad that didn't happen. I know that I turned to alcohol to try to numb my feelings and help me survive in many different social situations. I was able to laugh at myself if I was drunk and pretend that I didn't care. It helped my anxiety, which, at the time, I didn't even realize I had. When I was in college and throughout my life, I did not talk about anxiety or my feelings. I just smiled and pretended I was ok. **During my research about highly sensitive people, I learned that our nervous systems are extremely sensitive to alcohol and all types of drugs- including medicine.**

I remember the moment the doctor said I needed back surgery right away for a herniated disc in my back. My world turned upside down with that one statement. I was at a really great point in my life- other than my pain! My kids were one and three and, most importantly for me at the time- I had lost ALL of my baby weight! I was so proud of myself. I had gone to Weight Watchers and thought I had solved my weight issue forever. I was back down to my "normal" weight. Then I had back surgery. I was a Mom, wife, daughter, teacher. I had things to do and people to take care of. Back surgery took all that away from me and made me feel like nothing. I could barely be around my kids because of their energy. My back hurt every minute after surgery- worse than before the surgery. I had to move home and stay with my parents. I had to learn to accept help instead of being able to help others. I think the worst day for me was when I realized that I had to rely on other people. I had warmed up a piece of pizza for lunch and after eating, went to throw some of it away. I dropped a piece of pepperoni on the floor next to the garbage. I couldn't bend down to pick it up. My body would not allow me to do this. I cried. I had made a mess and couldn't even take care of myself. My identity at the time was consumed with taking care of others but this forced me to be the recipient instead of the giver. I went into a deep depression and had to crawl my way out. It forever changed me. I felt the pain I had while writing this book was a way for me to learn some of the same lessons I had learned after my

back surgery. I had to learn to listen to my body or the pain would get worse and
worse. I had to take better care of myself every single day.

My near death experience (NDE) in college most definitely was something I had
never spoken about before. After reading about Anita's NDE and several others, I was
aware that this was what happened that night.

Chapter 3 Faith

I cannot even begin to explain all of the "weird", "crazy" things that happened once I started writing this book. I started documenting them immediately after my trip. During the story, I felt the many different ways the universe/Spirit sent me messages. The songs were unending, especially while I was in Florida. I could rationalize that I hear a lot of uplifting music because I listened to the Christian station on Sirius XM radio. But, the fact that I was surrounded by all of these same songs- at the condo, on Facebook, etc.- I believe that was Divine Guidance speaking to me. I believe that I was so busy with life- my new job, losing my parents, and helping others that I wasn't always taking the time to notice messages from God. I had to learn to quiet my mind. The way I was able to get back in touch with Spirit was to be still- to learn to breathe, relax and make good choices of whole, real food. (more on this later!)

Faith is something I feel with my entire body. It is inside me. I felt it as a child and I still feel it today. I feel it when I quiet my mind and surrender to God's will. It's when my rational mind let's go of all of my beliefs and I am in the present moment. Just like the bird at the condo, I am who I am and I am where I am at in the present. No judgments. No preconceived ideas that I don't belong. Nothing. I just am. I imagine myself as a newborn baby- pure and beautiful. Every single part of myself. Even the things I don't like about myself. Everything is just as God made me.

"Meditation is simply a state of being in which the active mind slows down. It will bring you to a place where you can shut down. It will bring you to a place where you can shut down your mental chatter and become more aware of the subtle energies inside of you." ~John Holland

There are many ways I learned to quiet my mind. I sit quietly for at least five minutes and focus on my breath. I have to do this everyday to feel the benefits. By quieting my mind, my entire body relaxes and I feel very different. I am more present. I am more in line with my Spirit and my soul. Food affects my connection too. The more real food I eat, the more I am connected. The more processed food I eat (anything man made), the more "fuzzy" my brain feels. I don't think about things the same way and I am more apt to judge and be negative. Another way to quiet my mind is to exercise. I had to learn that exercise was what my body needed and not think of exercise or eating healthy as a way to get skinny. As an educator, I am passionate about doing more of this type of work in classrooms and with adults in the workplace. When adults are more relaxed, we are better equipped to handle the stress at work. And, when students are able to slow down and regulate their body, they are better able to learn. We live in such a busy world. I believe daily Mindfulness techniques should take priority for everyone.

My faith continues to be strong and it helps me every single day. Without it, I'm not connected to myself and I feel absolutely alone in a big world. I pray every day for myself and others.

Chapter 4 Death and Spirits

I am still learning about my connections with Spirits. I know that I can sense things that I can't see. It is like a psychic feeling or a sixth sense. At times I feel great about this and at times, it scares me. I understand now that this connection with Spirit is not about being an empath. It is something else I will continue to learn about. This connection is what makes me who I am and I am learning to accept that part of myself.

I am not sure why my mother didn't share information with me about my father's heart attack. I tried to put myself in her shoes and know that she did the best she could with what she was given. She might have been scared and worried that my father would die like her father did. She would be left alone to raise four children. I think that major life events like this always change us and nobody can truly understand until we live through it ourselves. Even then, everyone's situation is so different that it is impossible to all have the same experience.

I have had difficulty sleeping for years. I need the room totally quiet and no movement around me. I can't sleep with a dog, a cat or even my husband. I used to be quite embarrassed about this and didn't want anyone to know. Now, my husband and I joke about it with friends. Even though we are laughing, I sometimes feel awful about it. When I began reading about empaths and sleep, I realized that this was why I couldn't sleep. I was an empath and empaths struggle with sleep. There were other people like me out there.

"I personally have certain requirements when it comes to sleeping well. First and foremost the room must be pitch black with no visible light. Secondly, I require it to be deadly silent so you can hear a pin drop. And finally, I need my own bed." ~Marianne Gracie

I remember the night I read this. I told my husband, "It makes me feel better knowing that I am not some sort of freak! There is a reason I have so much trouble sleeping. I am an empath!" Of course, he would have no idea what I meant when I said that. Just reading this information helped me feel like I wasn't alone. I sleep in a totally dark room, with earplugs, a facemask and the door closed so I won't hear anything. I also learned how important sleep was for an empath's health. During the time I was in pain in the story, I wasn't sleeping and it was affecting my entire nervous system. When I healed and began sleeping again, I felt like a new person!

"Do you know what happens when you decide to stop worrying about what other people might think of you? You get to dance. You get to sing. You get to laugh loudly, paint, write, and create.You get to be yourself. And you know what? Some people won't like you. Some will laugh or mock or point out flaws...but it just won't bother you all that much." ~Doe Zantamata

Well, for me, I might not necessarily be dancing or singing, but I am sleeping! I find so many people nowadays struggling with sleep. I always wonder if they tried sleeping like I do, would it help them? With a good night's sleep, I am better able to handle what life throws at me.

Past life regression work is a healing technique that I have used to help some of the physical and emotional pain in my body. These regressions aren't just a therapy session. While writing this book, I was able to meet Brian Weiss. His story is so inspiring because he was a psychiastrist who did not believe in anything that wasn't science based. If he hadn't followed his intuition, I might not be following mine. I was able to say to him, face to face, "You changed my life." I meant it. He said to me, "Thank you for telling me that and thank you so much for coming today." It was genuine. He knew that by following his internal voice, he had changed my life. It didn't matter that he had changed thousands of lives. It mattered that he had changed my life. *That is what is helping me write this book. Can I change just one life? If so, then daring to share my story is so worth it. My story only took a few messages from Heaven. What will it take the next person? And the next? We all need to share our stories to heal the world, a voice encourages me.*

I remember the phone call from my sister-in-law about my nephew, Tyler. It was before cell phones so I answered the land line. My kids had friends over and I remember looking at all the kids as I walked to the garage, searching desperately for my husband. I was hearing the words and hoping for something different. As I listened to, "Tyler was in a car accident," I was hoping to hear, "he is ok. Banged up and in the hospital, but he will be ok." That is not the information I received. It was, "he died." My husband looks at me with fear in his eyes. He can see it in my eyes even before I hand him the phone. The kids all followed me to the garage. They are aware that something big, and most likely bad, is happening. I break the news to all of them. *How do I even explain something like this to my kids? I can't even understand it myself. We are all in shock as we sit down to talk. The rest of the day is a blur. I know we make plans to fly to Tyler's home town and we buy our boys their first suit to wear to the funeral. My kids would be so much younger (12 and 14) than I was when they attend their first funeral. I remember holding them as we cried together. As a Mom, I wasn't sure how to help them but I did the best I could.*

It was on the trip to my nephew's funeral a colleague recommended that I read Brian Weiss's book, <u>Many Lives Many Masters.</u> It was 2008. I was in the lobby of the hotel checking my email on the hotel's computer. A colleague had sent an email asking if I wanted to order a particular book to help with a class I was teaching. I responded something like this, "I'm sorry. I can't deal with this right now. I had to fly to Tennessee because my nephew was killed in a car accident. I'm not sure when I will be home. Thanks, Monica". She responded something like, "I'm so sorry to hear about your nephew. I read a really good book called *Many Lives, Many Masters* I think it might help you." The seed had been planted and forever my life would be changed by this one person daring to share information about souls, spirituality and healing through past life regression work. For me, it was foreign to have a professional colleague share such a new age/spiritual book. But it wasn't spiritual like religious. It was different. I don't know why but on the way home in the plane, I had the book *A New Earth: Awakening to Your Life's Purpose* by Eckartt Tolle. Eckartt introduced me to thinking more about why we are all here on this planet- like where I ask myself, *"Like why am I here on earth kinda why?"*

"What a liberation to realize that the 'voice in my head' is not who I am. 'Who am I, then?' The one who sees that." ~Eckartt Tolle

I have had the opportunity to work with Betty Moore Hafter (author of the foreword!) who was trained by Brian Weiss. I was able to access some past lives during several sessions. I am so grateful for this experience.

I remember the first time I ever tried a past life regression. During a regression, it is similar to a meditation where I close my eyes and a voice directs me through the process. First, the person directs me to relax every single part of my body, one part at a time. Then I visualize walking through a door and down a path. It is like I picture a movie in my head. Here is the story I thought about. I walk down a path. I am wearing leather sandals and a robe. My mind wanders and I begin to judge my thoughts. *I was scared that I wouldn't be able to do this because I wasn't sure I believed that this would work.* There are many other people at the place I am walking towards. There is a wooden cross, similar to the one Jesus was crucified on. *My brain thinks "What is going on? I couldn't be Jesus in a past life! But there were so many similarities!"* I ignore the thoughts and I continue walking. There are a lot of people screaming. Although I can't hear what they are saying, I can sense they are very angry. There are others dressed like me. At the end of the visualization, the voice directs me to skip to the end of this person's life. How did this person die? I proceed to talk about the pain in my wrists as someone nails me to the cross. As I die in this past life in my mind, I see my neck flail as the pain is released from my body. Then I am with God.

What? I'm sure you are questioning the truth of this story. Trust me. So did I. After the meditation, I was brought out of the hypnotic state and to the present moment in this lifetime. Were there any similarities in this lifetime? Only if I want to believe, I think to myself. I have had two wrist surgeries and continue to have pain in my wrists. *Was this left over from another lifetime? I would never be able to prove it to anyone, but what if?* I feel that I might be 'crucified' for being a public school educator who believes in God. *Well, maybe not crucified, but most definitely fired if I started teaching about my beliefs at the public school where I was a teacher or an administrator.* I had a difficult time accepting this experience as one of my past lives. That is, until one day a coincidence happened.

I had a difficult time believing because I felt like it was Christ's story and I knew I was most definitely NOT Christ in a past life. I did not know anyone else who was crucified on a cross. A few weeks later, my husband was channel surfing and happened to stop and watch a documentary about a religious community in another country. I stopped whatever I was doing to watch as they sacrificed people on crosses, just like Jesus. I remember clearly thinking, "Oh, someone other than Christ was crucified on a cross? I had no idea!" I was meant to see that 5 minutes of the TV show to help me trust that my story was real. *This one event would encourage me to go deeper and explore this alternative healing technique for many other pains in my body. It isn't like the pain goes away instantly but over the course of months it gets better and better until it finally releases from the cells in my body. Based on Brian Weiss's research and my own experience, I believe our body holds the pain in our cells from past life trauma.*

"I didn't realize yet that thinking is only a tiny aspect of the consciousness that we are, nor did I know anything about the ego, let alone being able to detect it within myself...The egoic mind is completely conditioned by the past. Its conditioning is twofold: it consists of content and structure." ~Eckhart Tolle

In my past life regression, I can hear my ego questioning everything that I was thinking. My ego wants to tell me it is my imagination running wild, but my subconscious wants to believe.

I am always amazed at the people I meet- both in and out of my profession. I always wonder what type of experiences brought each and every person to where they are in life. I wonder why they believe in this or that. Everyone brings to the table something different when talking about issues affecting our world. I'm sure that by reading this book, people will most likely think differently about the person who they thought I was. They might understand me or they might judge me based on what I have shared. Once introduced to new ideas, I knew my life had changed and everything up until this point helped me understand my path.

Chapter 5 Before the Dimes

It is normal for us to want to break away from our parents. It's part of our development. At age two or three, a baby starts to test the breaking away from his/her parents by walking further and further away. Then at about thirteen, we begin to realize that we don't have to believe everything our parents believe. Then at eighteen, we feel invincible and don't want to listen to most of our parents' advice. Since I was little, it seemed that my soul's quest was to always go against my mother- at every single age and stage. It was like I was born to live differently. I held on to things that happened to me as a child and tried to prove that I was right and she was wrong. I held on to my anger from her telling me to go back to bed on Mother's Day. I was never open to any of her attempts to connect with me. I built a shield to protect my heart from being hurt again. For example, when she tried to get me to watch Wayne Dyer, I wasn't receptive because I felt like she had hurt me before and I was trying to protect my heart even when I didn't need protection anymore.

In many parent-child relationships, a lot of people think the parent is supposed to teach the child. This is for things like learning to play baseball or learning how to cook. Nowadays, it seems the child is teaching the parent lessons. People are more open to talking about their feelings now more than when I was growing up fifty years ago. Each generation seems to be evolving more and more. We are changing the way we live by listening more to the children. My own children continue to teach me everyday.

Certain people I have met over the years have had an incredible impact on my life and it seems they might never know it. It can be a quick conversation, a professional relationship or a close friend. Certain things that people say resonate with me and guide me along in my life. I feel blessed and grateful for all who have entered my life to teach me things. Yes, even the negative people. They teach me who I don't want to be. These people help me look inside myself to see where I might need to be healed. I bless them and move on. Life is too short to stay in the negative. I truly want them to be happy.

That first video on vulnerability opened up new doors in my life. It triggered a domino effect for me to learn more and begin to admit my own insecurities. Brene Brown helped give me the courage to dive deep into myself to heal and then share my story. She helped give words to my feelings, validating them and helping me face them.

By sharing stories about her life, she helped me know that emotions and feelings were ok. They were part of being human. It was ok to be angry with my mom but then I had to learn to move beyond the anger.

Chapter 6 Messages and my Inner Voice

How about that guy working at the condo? I still have visions of him pointing to his head and saying, "I have to remember them in my brain." It was one of those "weird" or "crazy" things that began happening to me as I began to write this book. *Because of these signs, I knew that my soul was meant to write this book. I had to be willing to listen and move forward. When writing, I felt connected to the Spirit within me. Through eating clean, taking care of myself and opening up my heart, God guided me in the right direction. Just like God placed my husband and I outside the night we went to dinner, I would be placed with an opportunity to share my story.*

I knew about the many stages of child development through my education to be a teacher. I hadn't studied much about adults though. I was not aware that menopause was anything but hormones and hot flashes.

"Uncertain as I was as I pushed forward, I felt right in my pushing, as if the effort itself meant something. That perhaps being amidst the undesecrated beauty of the wilderness meant I too could be undesecrated, regardless of the regrettable things I'd done to others or myself or the regrettable things that had been done to me. Of all the things I'd been skeptical about, I didn't feel skeptical about this: the wilderness had a clarity that included me." ~Cheryl Strayed

I didn't realize that in menopause, along with the hot flashes, would come anxiety and an increase in my intuitive abilities. I would discover ways to help my anxiety. One was to be in nature as much as possible. The second was eating healthy. The third was making sure to exercise every single day, just like the doctor in the story. The more I did these things, the less anxiety I would have.

"We form at age 30, we transform at age 40, and we transmute at age 50."
~Barbara Hand Clow

I felt like I was in the middle of a life review, like in the book Life's Golden Ticket. Because of this, I experienced all of the emotions and feelings from everything that had happened to me in 50 years! I tried many supplements and medicines to try to feel better, but, eventually the thing that would help my anxiety and pain were writing this book and literally rewiring my brain. Like I thought in my younger years that I could find confidence in the bottle of alcohol, I thought I could heal my anxiety, menopause, and digestive issues with herbal supplements or a pill. That isn't how it works. Some medicine and supplements did help, but I had to do the tough emotional work too. *Through writing my story I was able to accept myself. Would I have written this story without the dimes? Most likely not. Would I have found another way? I have no idea, but am happy to be on this journey.*

"Research into the physiological changes taking place in the perimenopausal woman is revealing that, in addition to the hormonal shift that means an end to childbearing, our bodies-and, specifically, our nervous systems- are being, quite literally, rewired. It's as simple as this: our brains are changing. A woman's thoughts, her ability to focus, and the amount of fuel going to the intuitive centers in the temporal lobes of her brain all are plugged into, and affected by, the circuits being rewired." Dr. Christian Northrup

If you are over 40 and have not read Dr. Christian Northrup's book called *The Wisdom of Menopause: Creating Physical and Emotional Health during the Change,* do it now.

When I was in my twenties and had sinus infection after sinus infection, I went to an allergist to try to find the cause of all of my colds. I remember getting those results and as the doctor spoke to me, I remember thinking "hell no!- I will never live like that!" The tests revealed I was allergic to dust and basically everything outside, including trees, grass, pollen, everything. His advice was that I should buy an air conditioner so that I wouldn't have to open my windows, take medication every single day and I shouldn't be swimming, camping or doing other outdoor activities. Basically, give up my lifestyle and all the things that helped regulate my body. I turned to other answers, which included making my own herbs from weeds. I hoped that the herbs would heal my body so I wasn't having allergic reactions to the environment. Looking back, I wonder if these environmental allergies were related to my gluten and dairy sensitivities and, most likely had affected my breathing. By eating these foods, my body's immune system wasn't as strong. At the time, I ate a ton of wheat products! *I'll never be able to prove it because most medical doctors don't look at food as the culprit for many diseases or allergies. Was the flour producing more phlegm and affecting my immune system? I may never know the answer but today I can say that eating less flour definitely helps me breath better.*

When I eat gluten, dairy or a few other foods, I have to do what I call a recovery plan. I need extra vitamin C. I need to go have some lymph drainage done by either a massage therapist or a chiropractor to open up my ability to breathe correctly. I have to eat lots of vegetables and make sure to get extra sleep. No big deal, right? Well, I can usually handle eating those foods once in awhile but I can't do it for days. My body needs whole, healthy foods- no processed or man-made foods in order to feel good. I need a lot of protein in order to feel like my gut and brain are functioning properly.

Many authors note these same things for empaths or a highly sensitive person(HSP) (Dr. Judith Orloff, Marianne Gracie, etc.).

"Patients who suffer from these chronic inflammatory disorders feel their symptoms not only come from the gut but also from the brain, in the form of fatigue, "brain fog," and chronic pain." ~Dr. Emeran Mayer

Another thing that happens when I eat wheat, dairy or other processed food is I get brain-fog and it increases my pain. When I eat these things, I am ok if I have a little bit. If I am free of these foods, my pain level decreases immensely and I am able to focus better. I can also access my "inner voice" better. When I say inner voice, I mean I feel more connected to my inner self, my soul or my subconscious. It's the same way I feel when I hike. Eating the foods God gave us and being on the earth, feeling the energy of nature are some of the best things for my body.

I recently heard a mother and daughter talking about food. It was the day I had worked on this part of my book. It mimicked exactly what I was trying to write about. Here is the conversation I overheard:

Mom: "Oh, you can't eat that because of your diet, right?"

Daughter: "Mom, I'm not dieting. It isn't that I can't eat it. I choose not to eat it."

Mom: "But, you can't eat it right? Are you still trying to lose weight?"

Daughter: "Mom, I am not trying to lose weight. I am trying to be healthy. I choose not to eat white flour and sugar. It's not that I 'can't' have it. It isn't a diet. Do you understand that?"

Mom: "But, you won't eat it right? I was going to cook lasagna. But, you can't have that right?"

Daughter: "Mom, I don't eat things with white flour. I eat whole foods. You know, like fruits, vegetables and meat. I can eat something else. It's fine."

I felt this person's pain. She felt like she had to defend her choice to eat whole foods. *Why do I have to explain this to everyone? Why is eating 'differently' such a weird concept for everyone? Whole, real foods should not be what people consider different! Why don't people understand that our society is eating way too many flour products? Why aren't people eating the food that God gave us? You know- the things that grow on the Earth. Why do I need to explain my choices in eating real food? Food needs to be from earth, not a science lab. I noticed a big change in my taste buds once I turned to real food. I was busy eating things because they tasted good- like sugar, bread, etc. Once I removed those from my food choices, vegetables and fruit tasted delicious!*

I am always amazed at our grocery stores. Most of the "food" items could live on a shelf for close to fifty years. The only place I should be buying 'food' is on the outer edge of the store. One trip around the store- go down the produce aisle, the meat aisle at the back of the store and the dairy/egg aisle (which now includes almond and coconut milk!). Then I should be done shopping. Everything else in the store are 'food-like' items. They are things that man created using some food and chemicals. I don't have to read the label on a banana because it is real food. If I can't pronounce the ingredients, then the item is not food. For the most part, I have to go shopping every single week because the food I buy will spoil and I will need more. But that's ok with me because I know I am eating food that doesn't include chemicals.

My body is like an individual science experiment. I can read about how nuts are really good for me. So, I try eating nuts for snacks. Well, when my body doesn't like certain nuts it shows me by affecting my breathing, my skin(I get itchy) or my digestive system. I have to listen to my body and stop listening to all of the advice everywhere. Sound simple? It's not. I struggle with it every single day. I actually ask my body before I eat if it really wants me to eat whatever is in front of me. My gut will tell me with just a sensation. We are all so different and our food journey needs to be our own science experiment. Food affects everyone differently because it isn't just about the food, it's our thoughts that affect the entire body.

I read the book *The Mind-Gut Connection* while I was writing this book. In chapter one, the author speaks of treating the body "like a machine". I knew I had stumbled upon exactly what I had been thinking about for years, especially after the conversation with my father. It was like my father was sending me messages about taking care of my machine in a different way. *"This is important. Listen up and make the changes,"* *the voice inside me said. Was it from my father? Was it from my internal voice- the one who wants me to be me?*

"The machine model was useful in medicine for treating some diseases. But when it comes to understanding chronic diseases of the body and the brain, it's no longer serving us." ~Dr. Emeran Myer

This quote explains my beliefs that our thoughts affect our "machine." Through my healing over the years, I have more luck with alternative healing than I ever did with medical doctors. I continue to do a mixture of medical and alternative ways to heal, but ultimately it is Reiki, Network Chiropractic Care, massage therapy, acupuncture and looking within myself which heals me the most. Eating real food helps my body to function better, but I still need these other therapies.

"But regardless of what supplements you take and what kind of exercise you do, when all is said and done it is your attitude, your beliefs, and your daily thought patterns that have the most profound effect on your health." ~Dr. Christiana Northrup

Our internal thoughts are the most critical part of enjoying our human body.

Was I able to make the changes I wrote about in the dime story? I am trying the 90%/10%. I eat clean and healthy 90% of the time and will enjoy treats about 10% of the time. I thoroughly enjoyed my cake, maple cream pie and gluten free pizza on my 50th birthday. Even though the processed 'food' they use to make gluten free pizza affects me- it isn't as bad as flour based pizza. Will I eat cake at every birthday or anniversary party that I go to? Probably not. This is partly because I would be eating cake and treats so much that it feels like I have to go into recovery mode almost all the time.

Chapter 7 Come What May

"I was standing with one foot still in the living room and one foot in the room that would be my escape route out of the house."~Monica Morrissey

This sentence is how I have felt my entire life. I have always felt that I have had one foot on earth and one foot in Heaven. I had to learn to connect my experience on earth and my experience with Spirit. This part of me is my highly sensitive system. I would much rather spend my time with God and my angels than deal with some of the pain on earth. I had to learn to do both. *I always felt this inside but never wanted to share it with others because I thought people would think I was crazy. I still have one foot in both worlds, but I am working on balance. I have to balance both my root chakra and my crown chakra.*

I have been reading about how our emotions affect our physical body for over twenty years. I was amazed when I began talking to people that most were not aware of this information. I might mention reading a book from Hay House and so many people had never heard of Louise Hay or Wayne Dyer. I realized how lucky I was to have this knowledge but I also realized that it was my path and my path alone that would determine if I would be able to incorporate this into my life. When I began to tell people about my book and how I was using a self-publishing company developed by Louise Hay from the Hay House Foundation, it was clear other people didn't read as many books from Hay House that I did. Sharing my story would be like that one colleague who decided to share Brian Weiss's book with me when Tyler died. That one thing would totally change my life's journey. *Writing and sharing this book would also be one of the most daring things I could do as an empath! When I am ok with "Come What May", then I am in a good space.*

Chapter 8 Time with My Dad

Healing using Alternative Methods

I find it very interesting that I have to call this type of healing "alternative" instead of traditional. These should be called traditional methods because cultures around the world have been doing this for years! In America we have developed a medical system focused on using a pill or a drug to "fix" the problem within the body. "Alternative" methods try to get to the root cause of the problem and help the entire body- not a piece or part of the body.

"Bodily symptoms are not just physical in nature; often they contain a message for us about our lives- if we can learn to decipher it." ~Dr. Christian Northrup

Remember the phrases, "Eat like your life depends on it" and "Think like your life depended on it"? Those phrases are how I began to heal my body. While writing the dime story, I didn't share that I took a break from technology that week and it was a shock to see how this simple change affected my physical body. I discovered that I was "tech sensitive". After discovering I was an empath I knew that technology was affecting my nervous system more than the average person. When my father was sick, I had to be glued to my cell phone. Now that I didn't need to be next to my phone all day and all night, I realized that with every vibration or notification I received, it was stimulating the fight or flight response in my body. With every vibration, I worried that something bad had happened. I had been so busy over the last few years that my nervous system was depleted and overloaded. Removing technology helped me learn to go within myself and still my mind.

"Medicine and science never paid much attention to the malfunction of the brain that was the primary cause of all these problems." ~ Dr. Emeran Mayer

I was first introduced to trying to change my thought patterns by a chiropractor who I went to before my back surgery. I had a lot of ear and TMJ pain. I remember she would send me home with positive quotes to read. Something like,

"I hear with love. Harmony surrounds me. I listen with love to the pleasant and the good. I am a center for love." ~Louise Hay.

After my back surgery, I would discover that these were from Louise Hay's book, *You Can Heal Yourself.* This was the book that included the mirror activity where I had to look in the mirror and say truthfully, "I love you." Over the years I have looked up many symptoms to find out the message behind the pain. For instance, the 'cause' for ear pain was:

"Anger: Not wanting to hear. Too much turmoil. Parents arguing" ~Louise Hay.

Louise then has a positive thought to go along with the cause. Here is another one. Cause for Colds (respiratory illness):

"Too much going on at once. Mental confusion, disorder. Small hurts. 'I get three colds every winter,' type thinking." ~Louise Hay.

The positive thought to go along with the cause for colds is:

"I allow my mind to relax and be at peace. Clarity and harmony are within me and around me. All is well." ~Louise Hay.

I wonder if she is trying to say that we don't "catch" colds but we "think" colds? Think of all of the people who use wipes everywhere they go because they are so scared of germs. Not that we don't want to wash our hands, but could we possibly "catch" colds with our thinking?

As a teacher over the years, I have been sick a lot. I tried an experiment. Instead of worrying about all of the germs in my classroom, I began saying to myself and everyone, "I have been teaching so long now, I have built up my immunity and I tend to stay healthy!" I wanted to see what would happen. My words were important. Here is another internal voice I had tried, "I have been teaching so long now that I don't get colds anymore." The first voice is positive (healthy) and the other voice was negative (don't get colds). According to the book The Secret, the universe didn't hear the **"don't"** in "don't get colds. It heard, "get colds" because the universe is **always** positive. Nowadays I cringe when I hear someone say, "there is a virus going around. I hope I don't get it." *Do I still get colds? Absolutely! When was my last cold- most likely the last time I thought, "Oh my goodness- I hope I don't pick up germs from that sick person."*

In my new role as Curriculum Director, I wanted to share some of these ideas with teachers. The idea was that if teachers understood how our thoughts affect our learning, they might understand how important it was for educators to address students' emotions along with learning the curriculum. I organized a profession development day to show the movie Resilience to the entire staff at both schools in my district. The movie brought to light the ACE (Adverse Childhood Experiences)study. The ACE study identified ten different childhood experiences that affected a person's health, even into adulthood, including their life expectancy. Finally, there was a medical study that proved our emotions affect our health! My personal passion was now a part of my professional world. The seed had been planted and I would be able to encourage educators to learn to take care of their own bodies so that they were ready for the challenges of teaching. I introduced essential oils and Reiki to some teachers. I introduced EFT (Emotional Freedom Technique) tapping to people. I realized that I was now able to share my personal passion with others in my professional career. Teaching is sometimes exhausting but by learning how to take care of ourselves, we would be able to keep educating the next generation.

The seed had also been planted to begin doing mindfulness activities as part of the curriculum. If students were emotionally and physically regulated, then they would be ready to learn.

Reiki

"Reiki is a Japanese technique for stress reduction and relaxation that also promotes healing. It is administered by 'laying on hands' and is based on the idea that an unseen 'life force energy' flows through us and is what causes us to be alive. If one's 'life force energy' is low, then we are more likely to get sick or feel stress, and if it is high, we are more capable of being happy and healthy.

The word Reiki is made of two Japanese words - Rei which means 'God's Wisdom or the Higher Power' and Ki which is 'life force energy'. So Reiki is actually "spiritually guided life force energy." `Retrieved from` https://www.reiki.org/faq/whatisreiki.html

When I was healing from my back surgery, I went to a free Reiki clinic. The first time I ever received Reiki, I fell asleep. My body was so depleted back then. I was in a lot of pain from my back and I had two little kids. It was a difficult time in my life and Reiki began to help me. I was trained to a level II Reiki practitioner. I did the training mostly to be able to give myself Reiki. Giving Reiki to others helps me feel better too. I cannot explain what happens during Reiki, but there is most definitely a healing energy that occurs. For me, it makes me feel better and relaxes my entire nervous system. *When I shared Reiki with others, I got comments like, "I feel like a totally different person!" I have had Reiki practitioners who were better than others but I am so glad to have Reiki in my life.*

Years ago, I had the opportunity to have a photographer take my picture with a special camera that would show my "energy field". In other words, the picture would show colors surrounding me. The camera would leave the lens open a little longer to pick up on the subtle light energies surrounding me. This is called a person's aura or energy field. I always felt this and could sense people's aura, but didn't really understand much about it. As an empath, I learned how to control my aura, where I could extend my energy and I could draw back my energy. Depending on how far I extended my energy would determine whether or not I picked up someone else's energy.

These pictures would be my physical evidence that I was always searching for. I wanted something to help me understand what was happening so that I would be able to "verify" auras to other people. Here is a link to the website where the photographer explains the colors surrounding me. https://aurainsightsauraphotography.wordpress.com/2011/08/17/aura-photos-of-before-and-after-reiki-1/

The photographer (Ramona from Aura Insights) said things like, "angel guides who surround her", "psychic ability", "open mind", and "intuitive abilities". The photographer took pictures both before and after I had Reiki.

According to this photographer, the white symbolized angels and spirit guides surrounding me, letting me know they are with me to help me.

After I had Reiki, she wrote things like, "the session appeared to open her up to allowing even more psychic energy in!" The bright purple color had opened my crown chakra. This is my connection with Spirit, the part of me that wants to be in Heaven. This is something I have felt my entire life but didn't have words or knowledge to describe it.

This aura experience would be three years after Tyler had died and I had only begun to read books by Wayne Dyer and other authors. It would take me years to understand and change my thoughts about what words like psychic and intuitive really mean.

For a long time, I blocked this connection. I knew that I could sense energy around people but this experience validated that a person's essence goes beyond their physical body. While writing this book, I am now trying to get back in touch with this part of myself. The photographer writes, **"In both her throat and heart area she shows purple, which just emphasizes how she uses some pyschic ability when she communicates with others, and it comes right from her heart."** For people who know me well, I most definitely wear my heart on my sleeve. It goes right along with the part in the story where I say, "Do all things with love." A colleague who I used to work with said something to me when I saw her recently. I gave her a big hug and she said, "I always feel better when you are around." This meant a lot to me as it was quite the opposite comment I had experienced with that friend years ago. This person felt my love. This person knew me and knew that I only wanted the best for her. She knew my energy was filled with love. I won't be able to be a "jack-ass whisperer" but I will be able to be a "love- whisperer" for those who want to receive love. When I started sharing about my book and being an empath, most people weren't surprised. It was almost like everyone around me knew and understood my sensitivities before I understood them.

I am a Facebook user. I love it and hate it at the same time. I love the connection with friends, family and past students whom I don't get to see very often. I love watching my students and their families grow up. I love the inspirational quotes and posts from positive people. One post is very clear in my mind, "Just because you think it, doesn't mean it's true."~ author unknown. This kinda messed with my head. Until then, I believed everything I told myself. Then I started questioning every thought I had. Every feeling I had. I realized that most of my thoughts were related to my emotions and my life experiences. The reason I hate Facebook is because some people tend to only look at other people through their own experiences. I can never understand someone else's story because I haven't lived it. And nobody knows my story because they don't know all of my experiences. *For anyone who knows me, were you surprised by anything you read in my story? I think even my family didn't know some of the things I shared! Imagine a world where we all accepted each other and respected that we don't understand because we don't know the life of the other person. It's like we can only see in the windows to a person's house. We don't see everything inside.*

Here is my understanding of the nervous systems. The parasympathetic part of our nervous system is the "rest and digest" part. The sympathetic nervous system is the "fight or flight" part. Meditation helps the parasympathetic nervous system calm and relax the body. My sympathetic nervous system had been running the fight and flight in my body for about the past 4 years. It's meant for danger such as tigers and bears. We either decide to stay and fight or we run like heck to save ourselves. I learned at an early age to avoid things, thus activating the flight part of the nervous system. During the time I was caring for both of my parents, the sympathetic nervous system was working overtime and the parasympathetic nervous system was only relaxing during the few times when I was praying. I had to learn to relax. *Ultimately, this was part of my "cure" for all of my ailments throughout the years. I had to learn how to breathe and deal with my emotions instead of trying to get a pill to fix me.*

I was lucky enough to learn about Emotional Freedom Tapping (EFT) from the same person who helped me with my past life regression work, Betty Moore-Hafter from South Burlington, VT. (She wrote the foreward to this book!) EFT is so simple and easy. Anyone can learn and it is so helpful for dealing with and releasing our emotions in our bodies. It will help with any type of stress. I remember one time I had a really bad pain in my neck on my way to work. I tried to figure out what was bothering me and instantly I thought of someone at work who was a "pain in my neck". I tapped out how I felt about what had happened the day before at work and was able to go to work pain free. It relieved the pain in my neck and the anger from the day before. I was able to go into work with a whole new attitude. I even had a great attitude with the person who I thought was a pain in my neck!

Learning to relax sounds really simple but to a workaholic like myself, it's difficult. I have a hamster wheel inside my head that will not stop. As a teacher, I was always thinking of lessons and strategies to meet my students' needs. I wanted to be a creative and good teacher. I rarely used my plans from year to year because technology was changing and I wanted my students to love learning. I didn't want old, outdated lessons.

What I didn't understand, was that I needed to quiet my mind to help me find my inner, positive voice. This voice was also the voice that would help me step out of my comfort zone and write this book.

Remember the doctor in the story who made time to exercise? Well, everyone needs to make time to be quiet too. Our bodies need it- just as much as we need food and exercise.

I started small. I learned that it was important to do this every single day. The length didn't necessarily matter. It was that my nervous system got to relax on a regular basis. I am still learning and know that this will forever be a part of my life. *I wonder what our society would look like if everyone did this? What if we shut off our computers each night for thirty minutes and just focused on our breath? Would everyone sleep better? Would people treat each other better? Would everyone be less stressed? Would the fight or flight part of the nervous system be relaxed? Breathe, a voice reminds me.*

Chapter 9 Unexpected Surprises

Just to clarify- the books we found were not porn, as we think about sex books today. One was a chapter book, explaining the how-tos of sex- in full length paragraphs. The picture book had black and white drawings portraying different sexual parts of the human anatomy. The copyright dates were the 1940's.

I share the story of my Grandfather having bladder cancer because, embarrassing as it is, that is where most of my pain was while I was writing this book. In my bladder. I even had surgery to make sure I didn't have bladder cancer like my Grandfather. It was the Urologist who told me to keep taking more and more of the medicine. That one doctor wanted me to take a pill to cover up the pain. I can remember another doctor telling me once, "we don't have muscle relaxers, we have brain relaxers." Basically, by using drugs to "cure" me, this doctor was covering up my symptoms.

I was diagnosed with interstitial cystitis. I was encouraged to eat lots of flour products and little fruit, along with increasing the medicine. The thought was to have a low acid diet. Of course, looking back, I see that because I was an empath and sensitive to those foods, this was the absolute worst thing I could eat.

I had looked up to see what Louise Hay said was the emotional trigger and the positive affirmation for bladder pain.

"Bladder problems- Anxiety. Holding on to old ideas. Fear of letting go. Being *pissed off... I comfortably and easily release the old and welcome the new in my life. I am safe."*

No big surprise here, right? Just think about my entire story- the release and letting go of old ideas.

In this chapter, I introduced the idea of sugar and flour being addictive for some people. I had read David Gillespie's book *Sweet Poison, Why Sugar Makes Us Fat* and most recently had tried eating like Susan Pierce Thompson's book, *Bright Line Eating* suggests. I am still amazed that people are unaware of how broken our food system is. People do not understand how most Americans seem to be eating too much sugar and flour. This idea was first brought to light in the book , *The Saccharine Disease* by Surgeon-Captain Cleave. This doctor began the conversation that it was sugar causing most of the illnesses in the 20th century. When I read Susan's book, she pointed to brain research which showed that sugar is more addictive than cocaine. I remember reading about a rat study where the rats got fat from eating too much sugar or flour. I began to say mantras in my head, "I will not be like the fat rats. I will not be a fat rat."

Mainstream media doesn't show us this information because so many companies might go bankrupt if everyone stopped eating sugar and flour. Now, let's just be clear here. I am not talking the whole "carb" debate. I am talking about flour and sugar, which both look similar to cocaine when chopped up into a fine powder. Flour is sugar in disguise because our body turns flour into sugar. Both create havoc with my digestive and respiratory system because my system wants whole foods from earth. This is what happened to me- I was eating way too much processed foods and not enough foods from earth. Along with having a highly sensitive system, I had been overloading my system for years with "food like" man made products. When I clear my system of flour and sugar, I breathe better and my stomach feels better. That's my test. Clear and simple. 90% of the time I won't have this type of food, but 10% of the time I will thoroughly enjoy them! I am lucky that I don't feel that I am addicted to flour and sugar like I was to alcohol. But, I constantly have to monitor it. I focus more on protein, vegetables and fruits. There are so many different programs and diets out there. I am choosing to focus on "if it grows, I'll eat it". And, I listen to the person who has the best advice for me- my body.

Chapter 10 A Liberty Head Dime
for Everyone

"When you judge another, you do not define them, you define yourself."
~Wayne Dyer.

We all have our own stories and our own internal voices. My stories determine how I respond to everything in my life. I always try to remember that I can't see inside the whole person to understand why they do the things they do. Writing this book is like opening up the windows to my life. We are all doing the best we can with what we have been given. Everyone is allowed, "freedom of thought", which is the meaning of the Liberty Head dime.

Chapter 11 Thy Will Be Done: A Summer on the Lake

Eating well most definitely helps me feel connected to Spirit. I am able to receive messages when my body is functioning properly. I didn't realize how cloudy and disconnected I felt until I really started eating healthy. It usually takes at least one entire week to begin to feel more connected. This was the only way I was able to write this book. If I had food that didn't make me feel good, my thoughts were clouded by my ego and my writing was fake. When I reread sections written with ego, I had to go back and rewrite them. Basically when I ate crappy foods, I had crappy thoughts and those turned up in my writing.

"The beginning of freedom is the realization that you are not the possessing entity- the thinker. Knowing this enables you to observe the entity. The moment you start watching the thinker, a higher level of consciousness becomes activated." ~Eckhart Tolle

I reflected on my eating habits a lot during my vacation in Florida. I realized that I inhaled my food very quickly. I asked myself, *Why was I like this? Why was I always in a rush to gulp my food down?* I realized that my eating habits over the years were always hurried because I always had something else to do. As a teacher sometimes my lunch period would only be ten minutes due to emergencies or a student needing extra support. I realized this was how I ate all of my meals- in a rush to finish. I began observing other people eating. They took their time. Sometimes it might take twenty or thirty minutes to eat their meal. They would stop eating to talk. I ate and continued talking while I chewed. I seriously did not stop eating once I started. I needed to slow down everything in my life- from eating to walking to writing- everything- Just like the Sheriff reminding me to drive slower.

As a teacher and a Mom, I felt like I never had enough time to get everything done. Instead of being in the present moment, my head was always in the next moment or a past moment. The business manager at my new office had a sign posted in her office that read, "The quickest way to get something done is to do one thing at a time." ~ author unknown Seemed pretty simple! I thought I was one of the best multitaskers around. What I didn't realize was that by multi-tasking I wasn't in the moment. Looking back, I wish I had spent more time enjoying every day and every moment. *I couldn't go back in time but I could try to be more present in the moment with everything I did- even eating.*

"If you hold on to the hurt feelings, your energy will get drained. This makes it important to realize that you have the power to forgive others and feel better yourself, as a result." ~Vik Carter

Drinking lots of water is also important. I don't drink seltzer water very much because the carbonation affects my nervous and immune system. My body doesn't process it very well. I remember taking my Praxis exam to become an administrator. When I finished the exam, the gentlemen at the desk said, "Well, now you can go home and enjoy a glass of wine or a beer." I replied, "Thanks, but I don't drink alcohol." He apologized. I'm not sure why people say that. There is no need to apologize. Not drinking alcohol is my choice and I am happy with it. Anyways, he said, "Well, then, maybe enjoy a Coke or a Pepsi." I thought of how much sugar was in those drinks. Should I tell him I don't drink soda because of the sugar and carbonation? I did. He looked shocked. I didn't drink alcohol or soda. He looked at me and said, 'Well, what do you drink?" After my coffee first thing in the morning, I drink water with lemon or lime every day. It's the only thing my body really needs in order to function properly. *I don't think this made any sense to him.*

Chapter 12 Transitioning to Spirit

Thank you, God, for guiding me in helping my father transition to Spirit. I know You were with me helping me follow my intuition the entire time. I also know that when my dad left his physical body, he was changing form; he wasn't really gone. His soul continues his journey.

Chapter 13 The First Phone Call from Heaven

"Once an empath has better insight into people, places, events and situations that drain energy and ones that energize them, it becomes much easier to be selective in their day to day life." ~Vik Carter

I used to have a pair of boots that were my absolute favorite pair. They were tan colored, soft suede leather and they fit perfect. They had great arch support and went with a lot of my outfits. One year I didn't take very good care of them. They ended up getting wet in a pool of water from the melted snow. It ruined the leather. I tried and tried to fix them. Nothing worked. I couldn't wear them anymore. I wanted to go back in time and make sure to take better care of them. Of course, this was an impossible task but I still dream of those boots. The company doesn't make that particular boot anymore. I sometimes feel like this with relationships and some decisions. I made mistakes and didn't take good care of some of the relationships with people in my life. I did things that most likely damaged it forever. I couldn't go back in time and act differently. I had to move on and hope people would forgive me for some of my mistakes. I'm a different person now. I'm not the person who didn't understand how important it was to forgive and forget. Life can be like that- you have regrets and you want a re-do but time marches on. I was moving forward.

I used to be a planner. I planned everything and knew exactly what I would be doing each and everyday. When I started writing, I began to let life happen. When I did that, surprises came every day. My son would text me and and say he was stopping by my house. When I had thought I would be alone for dinner, he and his wife stayed for dinner. We ate something totally different than what I thought my dinner was going to be. I thought I would be eating leftovers alone. Unexpected surprises seemed to appear every single day. It was better than what I expected. I realized that I cannot plan everything in my future. I knew that I could set goals and work towards them, but ultimately it was God in the driver's seat. Just like being on the mountain. I had decided to hike the mountain, but God had planned something for me when I reached the top. Even this book wasn't planned by me. I never wanted to be a writer. In fact, as a teacher I didn't even like to teach writing!

I knew when Spirit was giving me messages during my writing. When this happened, it was like my linear brain (ego) let go. When my messages were coming from Spirit, I didn't know how to spell words and I didn't know how to use punctuation. Normally I am an extremely good speller and because I was a teacher, I was really good with punctuation. That part of my brain would shut off and I spelled simple words incorrectly. Wayne Dyer points out that there is a difference when you write from your soul versus just typing. I felt the difference as I continued to write.

"Start listening to the voice in your head as often as you can. Pay particular attention to any repetitive thought patterns." ~Eckhart Tolle

Chapter 14 The First Dime from Heaven

Writing this chapter was surreal. I can picture myself on the mountain, all alone on a sunny fall day. I know I was crying but had so much on my mind that I was barely in the moment. I can picture that dime in the dirt. I am glad I was on the phone with Merrilee because I was able to share with her one of the most precious times in my life. I knew this was my father reaching out to me. It helped guide me when taking care of his estate. I decided to make another necklace with that dime. Forever it will be with me and part of the reason I wrote this book.

The dead pens were an amazing way to send a message. I had to be ready to listen to all of the signs. I had spent a good part of my life covering up this part of me in order to survive in a tough world. *I had to believe and feel connected to Spirit in order for the universe to begin sending the messages.*

Chapter 15 Messages

    Numbers continue to show me signs every single day. There were too many to put in Part II of the book. I highlighted all of the 8's in the story because that was Tyler's uniform number.

Chapter 16 Life Marches on

This book is most definitely one of the biggest unexpected surprises of my life. I never dreamed I would ever become a writer. Once I started writing, I truly felt my soul opening up and I began to heal through the process. Without my Master's classes, I'm not sure I would have done this. The professors who worked with me forever changed my life. Not just with new credentials so I could get a new job, but they helped me discover my why- like "Why am I here on earth kinda why."

The camp foundation was the only part that was saved from our family camp. I think of foundations like childhood. My foundational beliefs were part of who I am, but I am constantly rebuilding them. I can change my body and my thoughts. I don't have to carry with me all of the parts of a foundation, but it does give me a starting point for life. I have the ability to change my life whenever I want. Sometimes it can be slow changes or I can tear it all down and start totally new. It's my choice.

I had a foundation of God within me from my childhood, but because organized religion had taught me some things, I wasn't always sure of myself. I had to let go of some of my childhood beliefs to understand that it was ok to believe in the things that I was being exposed to. Especially being an empath. My foundation was that I knew we were all different but I never knew about empaths or highly sensitive people. Now that I know, my life can be a new adventure!

The dreams I shared in the dime story helped me so much during those stressful times when I was worried. While writing this book, I happened to see one of my mother's cousins, Mary Redman. She was a tutor at the school I worked at. I hadn't seen her for years. She asked how everything was going and then asked about the family camp. When people do this, I always feel bad that we had to sell it. Mary remembers all of the Allen family reunions we had at camp with all of my mother's cousins and kids. The reunions are always a precious memory for everyone. So, instead of being negative, I shared the story of the dream I had where Dad showed me the photo album. I wanted Mary to know that we will always have those memories. Then she shared about one of her dreams.

Mary's husband, Paul, had passed away a few years ago. (I think it was when I was living with my Dad.) Mary shared that Paul organized a lot in the house so when he was gone, she had to figure some things out herself. She went to the bank to open the safety deposit box and didn't realize that Paul had the other key she would need to open the box. She went home and searched all over, including the desk where he kept everything. She got so angry and frustrated that she screamed and said, "Paul, you need to tell me where that key is right now!" She went to bed that night and he came to her in a dream, just like my mom and dad did with me. Mary told me that he laughed at her just like he always used to do and then said, "Mary, you know right where it is. It is in the drawer of that other table." Mary woke up, walked over to the drawer and there was the key. *Even though I know she misses her husband, I also saw the smile on her face. I know she felt he was connecting with her from Heaven.*

Chapter 17 THE Dime

"Being is not only beyond but also deep within every form as its innermost invisible and indestructible essence. This means that it is accessible to you now as your own deepest self, your true nature. But don't seek to grasp it with your mind. Don't try to understand it." ~Eckhart Tolle

Can you believe it? The EXACT type of dime from my father's collection? I found three coins in that house. First, a regular dime, then a penny and then a Liberty Head dime. At times, it feels surreal. Other times, I feel both of my parents nearby. Writing this book was most definitely a journey of my soul.

"You need to trust that there are parts of the creative process you cannot see, parts that work in mysterious ways, guided by whatever you want to call it- your unconscious, your muse, your higher power. You need to remember this because, with faith, you will find a way to do the work necessary to manufacture meaning out of material. Without faith, another unfinished project is likely to end up in the abyss of your bottom drawer." ~Joni B. Cole

While writing this book, I had to go within myself to find out why I had such a difficult time dealing with my mom. I realized that it wasn't her. It was me. I was built differently and none of us understood it because we didn't have the information. Not only am I an empath absorbing other people's feelings, but I am intuitive or psychic. I am still on this journey to discover exactly what this all means. I am not hiding this part of me anymore. I am learning to accept that because of my system being built differently, I have to take care of myself every single day. I have to use all of the skills I have learned. From meditation, to eating whole foods, not judging others, praying for those who hurt me, listening to my body and much, much more. Forever and always, life will be More Than a Dime, but the dimes showed me that we are connected to another realm, one that we can't physically see but we can believe in it just like the invisible breeze that blows the leaves. It's the life essence and energy that guides us in this spiritual journey as a human being.

One of my favorite things to do now is to drop dimes and pennies wherever I go. I imagine that when I drop a dime or a penny, I am sprinkling love. I imagine the person picking it up and feeling a bit closer to their loved ones in Heaven. Dropping dimes helps to heal my heart.

A few years before my parents passed away, I gave them one of the best gifts ever. Instead of a Christmas present, I gave them an Advent Story Calendar that I created. Every day for December they would open up a different envelope in the box I made. Inside the envelope was a story written by myself, my siblings or their grandkids. The story was a favorite memory about my parents. Here was one of mine:

"I loved having Christmas downstairs. Of course, at first, it was very important that Santa have a chimney where he could come into our house. It was always cozy to have the fireplace going and especially putting in the things that made the fire have different colors! It was always fun to open all of our presents down there. Of course, I thought I was dead meat when I got caught sneaking down to see my presents in the middle of the night. The biggest joke was definitely on me since

I never knew it was DAD who set the traps, including the tin cans that made a loud rattle sound. I thought I woke up everyone in the whole house! I loved the year I got my new water skis because I knew then I could be like the "big kids"!

~Monica"

The Advent Story Calendar helped us all remember the positive memories. It's so easy to blame and focus on the negative. This idea was the best thing at the time for Mom and Dad. I'm happy that my parents were my parents. It made me who I am today. Whenever I see people who knew them, they always remind me how kind my parents were.

A young mother and friend recently wrote a post on Facebook and I felt it would be a perfect ending for my book. Here is what she said:

"Talking with a coworker yesterday about an activity she had planned with her kids for this weekend. She excitedly said "I am the best mom ever" and paused, looked at me and continued with "for my kids, and you are the best mom ever for your children." We both kept working, but I couldn't help but reflect on what she had said. How much truth was behind her words? These days it is so easy to become discouraged as a mother. Maybe you weren't able to breastfeed your child as long as you had wanted, your body just didn't cooperate. So maybe you had a c-section and had hoped to have an all natural birth. Only got 6 weeks maternity leave where some mothers are lucky enough to stay home and watch every second of their child grow and learn. I could go on and on but the point is as mothers we give so much of ourselves for these tiny little people, who steal our hearts at first sight. We put ourselves last, lose countless hours of sleep, drain every ounce of our bodies, and I'm sure I'm not the only one who feels like they just aren't enough at times. But we are! We are mothers! We grow people, and that's pretty freaking amazing. We are the best, and there is no doubt about that! I hope my mama friends who read this smile and reflect on how amazing you really are. And I hope you never forget, YOU are the best mom for your children! ❤" ~Kayley Griffin

We are all perfect- exactly the way we are. I know I am doing the best I can with my life and so is everyone else. We are also trying to be the best parents we can. Are we all perfect? Absolutely not! We are all humans doing the best we can.

When I began telling my dime story and began sharing about my book, people from all over began sending me pictures of dimes and telling me stories about connecting with people in Heaven. The dime made them think of me but more importantly, it made them happy, which is truly what I want for everyone in this world. I love hearing stories from other people. It connects us.

"At midlife our hearts ask us to wake up and live our personal truth so that there is a seamless connection between what we say we believe and how we actually live our day-to-day lives." ~Dr. Christian Northrup

In order to heal, I had to learn to connect my gut, my brain and most of all, my heart.

When I left Lakeview Union Elementary School to take a job at Hazen Union as a Middle School Math teacher, a colleague gave me a book. The book is called Miss Maple's Seeds. Inside the front cover, she wrote, "Monica- For all the 'seeds' you nurtured into 'beautiful plants'- Best Wishes on your new endeavor. ~Carrie ;) " When she wrote this, she would have no idea that her niece, Samantha, who passed away so suddenly would be planting a sunflower in my garden each and every year. I hope this book has planted some "seeds" of thoughts. I wish everyone the best as we all discover our life lessons and some sort of connection to the universe. Here are some of the authors who planted seeds in my mind. Check out my Resources to see all the authors who planted seeds in my mind!

How does all of this relate to education? We have an educational system built on a factory model that teaches to the linear brain. As humans, we have a need to learn how our hearts affect our ability to learn. Kids cannot learn like a robot. We need to be able to teach to the heart and the brain at the same time. We need to teach students how to regulate their bodies and deal with the stress they feel inside. By remembering our human characteristics, educators will be able to help children grow and develop into happy, healthy citizens. We will be able to help them get over their fear of making a mistake in front of their peers. We will be able to teach them about how our bodies function to better support them in the classroom. Might this topic be another book?

Resources/Bibliography

When I was young, I never wanted to read. It wasn't until I discovered Judy Blume's book, Are You There God? It's Me, Margaret that I started reading. After reading this book, often times I would think, " Are you there God, it's me, Monica." As an adult, I never read much until that first Brian Weiss book led me to Hay House Publishing. I had found "my books". These were all about real people with real lives. These books helped explain what I felt inside. They put me in touch with God in a different way than organized religion did. Of course, a few beach romance novels here and there were always a good way to relax, but I wanted to read about real people with real connections with God.

As Brene Brown so nicely says, **"As neuroscientist Antonio Damasio reminds us, humans are not either thinking or feeling machines, but rather feeling machines that think."**

These books made me think about my feelings. They all have helped me grow as a person.

Here are the many resources that I have used to guide me in my journey of life. Happy reading!

1. *A course in miracles: Combined volume.* (2007). Mill Valley, CA: Foundation for Inner Peace.
2. Albers, S. (2009). *50 ways to soothe yourself without food*. New Harbinger Publications Inc.
3. Albom, M. (2018). *Five People You Meet In Heaven*. S.l.: Hachette Books.
4. Albom, M. (2009). *Have a Little Faith*. Detroit: Thorndike Press.
5. Albom, M. (2018). *The first phone call from heaven*. Leicester: Thorpe, Isis.
6. Albom, M. (1962). *The Timekeeper*. New York, NY: Hyperion.
7. Alexander, E. M.D. (2014) *The Map of Heaven*. New York. Simon and Schuster Paperbacks.
8. Altucher, J. (2013). *Choose yourself* (1st ed.). United States: Lioncrest Publishing.

9. Alvarez, M. (2012). *365 ways to raise your frequency: Simple tools to increase your spiritual energy for balance, purpose, and joy*. Woodbury, MN: Llewellyn Publications.

10. Andrews, A. (2009) *The Noticer* Sometimes, all a person needs is a little perspective. Nashville, Thomas Nelson.

11. Andrews, T. (2006). *Animal-speak: The spiritual & magical powers of creatures great & small*. Woodbury, MN: Llewellyn Publications.

12. Angelou, M. (2009). *Celebrations rituals of peace and prayer*. London: Virago.

13. Angelou, M. (2008). *Letter to my daughter*. New York: Random House.

14. Angelou, M. (1993) *Wouldn't Take Nothing For my Journey Now*. New York. Random house.

15. Berger, W. (2016). *A more beautiful question: The power of inquiry to spark breakthrough ideas*. New York: Bloomsbury.

16. Bernstein, G. (2015). *Spirit junkie: A radical road to self-love and miracles*. Retrieved May 2, 2018.

17. Blue Mountain Press. (2001). *Always follow your dreams, wherever they lead you*. Boulder, Colo.

18. Bolman, L. G., & Deal, T. E. (2011). *Leading with soul: An uncommon journey of spirit*. San Francisco, CA: Jossey-Bass.

19. Braden, G. (2008). *The spontaneous healing of belief: Shattering the paradigm of false limits*. Carlsbad, CA: Hay House.

20. Brown, B. (2018). *Braving the wilderness: The quest for true belonging and the courage to stand alone*. Retrieved April 7, 2018.

21. Brown, B. (2017). *Rising Strong How the Ability to Reset Transforms the Way We Live, Love, Parent, and Lead*. Retrieved April 19, 2018.

22. Brown, B., & Fortgang, L. (2015). *The gifts of imperfection*. Center City, Minnesota. Hazelden Publishing.

23. Brown, B. (2018). Listening to shame. Retrieved from https://www.ted.com/talks/brene_brown_listening_to_shame

24. Brown, B. (2018). The power of vulnerability. Retrieved from https://www.ted.com/talks/brene_brown_on_vulnerability?

25. Burchard, Brendon. (2008) *Life's Golden Ticket A Story About Second Chances*. New York, NY. Harper One.

26. Burpo, T. (2011). *Heaven is for real*. New York: Gale Cengage Learning.

27. Byrne, R. (2016). *The secret*. New York: Atria Books.

28. CAUDILL, M. A. (1995). *MANAGING PAIN BEFORE IT MANAGES YOU*. S.l.: GUILFORD.

29. Chopra, M. (2016). *Living with intent: My somewhat messy journey to purpose, peace, and joy*. New York: Harmony Books.

30. Coffin, W. (2005) *letters to a YOUNG DOUBTER,* Louisville, Kentucky; Westminister John Knox Press.

31. Cole, J. B., & Baer, H. (2017). *Good naked: Reflections on how to write more, write better, and be happier.* Hanover: University Press of New England.
32. Coyle, D. (2013). *The talent code.* New York: Bantam Books.
33. Courteney, H. (2010). *Countdown to coherence: A spiritual journey toward a scientific theory of everything.* London: Watkins.
34. Dale, C. (2010). *Everyday clairvoyant: Extraordinary answers to finding love, destiny, and balance in your life.* Woodbury, MN: Llewellyn Publications.
35. Daniel, C. (2016). *Bioenergy healing: Simple techniques for reducing pain and restoring health through energetic healing.* Retrieved December 15, 2017.
36. Dyer, W. W., & Hicks, E. (2017). *Co-creating at its best: A conversation between master teachers.* Retrieved May 18, 2016.
37. Dyer, W. (2010). *The Shift.* Hay House Publishing.
38. Farmer, S. (2006) *Animal Spirit Guides.* New York City. Hay House, Inc.
39. Frankl, V. (1959). *Man's Search for Meaning.* Boston. Beacon Press
40. Gillespie, D. (2008). *Sweet poison.* Penquin Books.
41. Grout, P. (2013). *E 2 Nine Do-it-Yourself energy experiments that prove your thoughts create your reality.* New York City, NY: Hay House.
42. Gracie, M. (2017). *EMPATH A Comprehensive Guide for Emotional Healing, Self-Protection and Survival for Empaths & Highly Sensitive People.* Retrieved July 9, 2018.
43. Hanson, R., PH.D., & Mendius, R., MD. (2009). *Buddha's Brain, the Practical neuroscience of happiness, love and wisdom.* Oakland, CA: New Harbinger Publications.
44. Hay, L. L., & Kramer, J. (2012). *Gratitude: A way of life.* Carlsbad, CA: Hay House.
45. Hay, Louise L. (1984) *You Can Heal Your Life.* Carlsbad, CA; Hay House, Inc.
46. Hicks, E & J. (2007) *The Astonishing Power of Emotions Let Your Feelings Be Your Guide.* Carlsbad, CA. Hay House, Inc.
47. Holland, J., & Pearlman, C. (2007). Born knowing: A mediums journey-- accepting and embracing my spiritual gifts. Carlsbad, CA: Hay House.
48. Holland, J. (2018). *Bridging two realms: Learn to communicate with your loved ones on the other-side.* Carlsbad, CA: Hay House.
49. Hunt, J. (2009) *Building Your Leadership Resume Developing the Legacy That Will Outlast You.* Nashville, TN. B & H Publishing Group
50. Hyatt, M. (2012). *Platform.* Nashville, Tenn.: Harper Collins Leadership.
51. Jones, R. (2013). *I am More Than Enough: Helping women Silence Their Critic and Celebrate Their Inner Voice.*
52. Junger, A., Greeven, A., & Witkowska, M. (2011). *Clean.* Warszawa: MT Biznes.
53. Knight, S. (2016). *The life-changing magic of not giving a f**k: How to stop spending time you dont have doing things you dont want to do with people you dont like.* London: Quercus.

54. Liptak, J. J. (2010). *2012--catalyst for your spiritual awakening: Using the Mayan tree of life to discover your higher purpose*. Woodbury, MN: Llewellyn Publications.

55. *Living sober*. (1975). New York: Alcoholics Anonymous World Services.

56. Macleod, A. (2010). *The Transformation Healing Your Past Lives to Realize Your Soul's Potential*. Boulder, CO: SoundsTrue.

57. Mass, W. (2010). *Every soul a star*. Retrieved December 1, 2013.

58. Mayer, E. A. (2018). *The mind-gut connection: How the hidden conversation within our bodies impacts our mood, our choices, and our overall health*. New York: Harper Wave.

59. Meyer, J. (2002). *Never lose heart: Encouragement for the journey*. New York, NY: Warner Books.

60. Moorjani, A. (2015). *Dying to be me: My journey from cancer, to near death, to true healing*. New Delhi, India: Hay House India.

61. MOORJANI, A. (2017). *WHAT IF THIS IS HEAVEN?: How our cultural myths prevent us from experiencing heaven on earth*. S.l.: HAY HOUSE.

62. Myss, C. (1997). *Why People Don't Heal and How They Can*. New York, NY: Three Rivers Press.

63. Niemeier, S., & Dirven, R. (1997). *The language of emotions: Conceptualization, expression, and theoretical foundation*. Amsterdam: J. Benjamins.

64. Northrup, C. (2018). *Dodging energy vampires: An empaths guide to evading relationships that drain you and restoring your health and power*. Retrieved May 2, 2018.

65. Northrup, C. (2012). *The wisdom of menopause: Creating physical and emotional health during the change*. New York: Bantam Books.

66. Notaras, K. (2018). *The book you were born to write* (1st ed.). Carlsbad, CA: Hay House, Inc.

67. Orloff, J. (2015). *The Power of Surrender*. Retrieved June 2, 2018.

68. Orloff, J. (2014). *The ecstasy of surrender: 12 surprising ways letting go can empower your life*. Retrieved June 2, 2018.

69. Orloff, J. (2005). *Positive energy: 10 extraordinary prescriptions for transforming fatigue, stress and fear into vibrance, strength and love*. Retrieved June 2, 2018.

70. Orloff, J., Dr. (n.d.). *Guide to Intuitive Healing 5 steps to physical, emotional, and sexual wellness*. Retrieved 2018.

71. Orloff, J. (2010). *Second sight: An intuitive psychiatrist tells her extraordinary story and shows you how to tap your own inner wisdom*. Retrieved May 30, 2018.

72. Osteen, J. (2017). *Become a better you: 7 keys to improving your life every day*. New York: Howard Books.

73. Osteen, J. (2006). *Scriptures and meditations for your best life now*. New York: Faith Words.

74. Peirce, P. (2011). *Frequency: The power of personal vibration*. New York: Atria Books.

75. Piper, D., & Murphey, C. (2015). *90 minutes in heaven: A true story of death & life*. Grand Rapids, MI: Revell.

76. Rothstein, D., & Santana, L. (2014). *Make just one change: Teach students to ask their own questions*. Cambridge, MA: Harvard Education Press.

77. Ruiz, M., & Wilton, N. (2012). *The four agreements: A practical guide to personal freedom*. San Rafael, CA: Amber-Allen.

78. Ruiz, M., Ruiz, J. L., & Mills, J. (2011). *The fifth agreement: A practical guide to self-mastery*. San Rafael, CA: Amber-Allen.

79. Rushnell, S. (2001) *when GOD winks How the Power of Coincidence Guides Your Life*. New York. Atria Books.

80. Sartori, P., & Walsh, K. (2017). *The transformative power of near-death experiences: How the messages of NDEs positively impact the world*. London: Watkins.

81. Schaub, E. O. (2014). *Year of no sugar: A memoir*. Naperville, IL: Sourcebooks.

82. Schwartzberg, L & MJRaval. (2014) *MINDFUL INTENTIONS*. New York. Hay House, Inc.

83. Segal, I. (2014). *The secret language of your body: The essential guide to health & wellness*. Glen Waverley, Victoria: Blue Angel Publishing.

84. Simon Sinek: Find Your Why | One of The Best Speeches Ever. (2018). Retrieved from https://www.youtube.com/watch?v=YnBs6YGPAu4

85. Sinek, S. (2018). *Leaders eat last*. Portfolio Penguin.

86. Sinek, S. (2016). *Together is Better A Little Book of Inspiration*. New York, NY. Portfolio/Penguin

87. Thielke, J. (n.d.). *The SLEEP Learning system Instant Pain Relief, Create Healing Energy*. Retrieved December 15, 2017.

88. Tolle, E., & Tolle, E. (2011). *Practicing the power of now: Essential teachings, meditations, and exercises from the power of now*. Sydney: Hachette Australia.

89. Tolle, E., & DiCarlo, R. E. (2016). *The power of now: A guide to spiritual enlightenment*. London: Yellow Kite.

90. Virtue, D. (2007). *How to hear your angels*. Carlsbad, CA: Hay House.

91. Virtue, D. (2011) *The Angel Therapy Handbook*. New York. Hay House Inc.

92. Virtue, D. (2010). *The crystal children*. London: Hay House.

93. Weiss, B. L., & Weiss, B. L. (2002). *Many lives, many masters ; Messages from the masters*. New York: One Spirit.

94. Weiss, B. L., & Weiss, A. E. (2013). *Miracles happen: The transformational healing power of past-life memories*. New York, NY: HarperOne, an imprint of HarperCollins.

95. Weiss, B. L. (2005). *Same Soul, Many Bodies: Discover the Healing Power of Future Lives through Progression Therapy*. Riverside: Free Press.

96. Wheeler, E. (2013). *Miss Maple's seeds*. Nancy Paulsen Books.

97. Zukav, G. (2010). *Spiritual partnership: The journey to authentic power*. New York: HarperOne.

Websites:

https://www.ask-angels.com/spiritual-guidance/angels-and-numbers/

https://aurainsightsauraphotography.wordpress.com/2011/08/17/aura-photos-of-before-and-after-reiki-1/

https://exemplore.com/paranormal/What-is-an-Empath-Traits-signs-solutions

https://hsperson.com/

https://www.huffingtonpost.com/tree-franklyn/youre-not-an-alien-youre-an-empath_b_7763702.html

https://www.carl-jung.net

https://www.reiki.org/faq/whatisreiki.html

https://aurainsightsauraphotography.wordpress.com/2011/08/17/aura-photos-of-before-and-after-reiki-1/

https://www.thebetterhealthstore.com/043011_top-ten-toxic-ingredients-in-processed-food_01.html

http://sensitive-theuntoldstory.vhx.tv/

https://day2dayparenting.com/help-child-learn-self-regulation/

https://ravenstarshealingroom.wordpress.com/2017/03/26/the-metaphysics-of-sciatic-and-peripheral-pain/

Monica lives in Northeastern Vermont with her husband. She has two sons and two grandsons. Monica taught elementary and middle school for twenty-seven years before changing careers to be a Curriculum Director. Now retired from education, she is a Master Reiki Practitioner, Inspirational Speaker, Past Life Regression Hypnotist, Health and Life Coach, and Intuitive Angel Card Reader. She enjoys helping people transform their lives.